PLAIN WORDS

TO

YOUNG MEN.

By AUGUSTUS WOODBURY.

CONCORD:
EDSON C. EASTMAN.
1858.

CONCORD, N. H.:
PRINTED BY McFARLAND & JENKS.

INTRODUCTION.

The substance of this volume consists of a series of Practical Lectures, delivered in the Westminster Church, Providence, R. I., during the winter months of 1857–8. They were intended more particularly for the young men who were connected with the congregation worshipping in that church. I have thought it best, at the solicitation of friends, to give them a wider circulation, by embodying them in the present volume. The young men of Lowell, Mass., will doubtless recognize a portion of these Lectures as delivered in the Lee Street Church, in that city, a few years ago. I trust, also, that I may not appeal in vain to the friendship of the young men of Concord, N. H., who have afforded me many pleasant associations. So, with the hope that these "Plain Words" will be read with favor and profit by those for whom they were written, I send out my little book, to meet with whatever fate it may deserve.

I have also added to the Lectures an Address delivered at North Granville, N. Y., July 29, 1857, on the "Position, Duties and Claims of Woman."

CONTENTS.

LECTURES.

I. INTRODUCTORY.

In introducing a course of Practical Lectures to Young Men, I wish to bear in mind, and to have it borne in mind, that I speak as a friend and counsellor, more than as a preacher. I would address myself as a young man to young men; one who knows their temptations, who has felt the pressure of their needs, and who understands their position. The main purpose which I have in view is, to turn the faculties of youth in the right direction — that they may engage themselves on the side of justice, of right, of liberty, and of religion, and that they may be occupied in the furtherance of all the best and noblest objects of life. The Lectures are designed to be thoroughly practical in their nature, dealing with the subjects proposed in the simplest and plainest way.

The Lecture this evening, as preliminary, will be devoted to the consideration of the Duty which a Young Man owes to himself, in the Use of the Opportunities which he possesses, in our Age and Country, and the Demands which are now made upon him.

Let us consider, briefly, the position of young men at the present day. It is not too much to say, that the present generation of young men occupy a position most important, as being those who are to determine the history of the future. There are great events at hand in the life of mankind, greater than any which the fathers knew. Old ideas are passing away; new ideas are coming on, to affect the whole condition of the human race. They apply themselves to all the various departments of human thought and labor; they enter into every scheme of business and government, and, in their development, affect all ranks of men. For the application of these ideas, the young men are the instruments. The old are gradually yielding their places, and retiring from active life. The young are coming forward to do the work which remains. The young, fresh, vigorous life which they infuse into social forces is needed to give new and stronger power to those forces, and employ them for the welfare of the race. "Old men for counsel," says the proverb, "young men for action!" The sage experience which has tested the various influences and powers of life, and knows what they are all worth, must come to give its counsel. We would not by any means disparage it. It tempers and restrains; it is prudent and cautious. But we need something more. Prudence is not the only virtue, and caution oftentimes loses the advantage. A railroad train furnished only with brakes would make but little progress, though brakes are very necessary articles. We should never despise the teachings of experience. But there are daily exigences arising, for which experience furnishes no rules, and we have to take counsel of the present rather than of the past, as we do the work we have in hand with all our might, as it demands of us to-day. Young men for action, in the stirring scenes of the present, taking the opportunity as it comes, using it faithfully and righteously, and leaving the result with a wise Providence!

It is evident that no grander opportunities have ever been given to any generation than those which belong to the present time. The general diffusion of intelligence — the application of knowledge to the useful arts — the quickened activity of the human mind, arising from the various influences of easier communication—of freedom from the drudgery of labor—of the accelerated speed of our material progress — and of the continual increase of material good, all have their effect, not only upon the condition but also upon the character. We are obliged to think faster, to feel more fervently, to comprehend more rapidly, as well as to work more swiftly. If we delay; if we hang back at all; if we stop to consider and carefully weigh what we shall do, we are left behind. The world passes by us. We are forced to think at the moment, and act as we think, or we lose our place in the general movement, and are soon forgotten. This is inevitable, as we go forward and take the place of action that belongs to us. The period of youth, therefore, becomes the period of preparation. We must, as young men, make ourselves ready, by daily cultivation of our best faculties, for that which the future has for us to do. We have to learn what is just and true, that, when the emergency demands it, we may take our position at once, and maintain it with that confidence in the righteousness of our convictions, which is one of the best assurances of success. There may be danger, it is true, that we shall form our opinions hastily. But even that danger will be obviated if we keep our loyalty to the great spirit of Truth unswerving, and are never false to what we firmly believe to be right. We have to keep our eyes open to see, and our ears open to hear, what the world is doing, that we may lose nothing by our neglect or indolence, but that we may be completely furnished for every work that may come. It is true, that now young men have a secondary place; but it will not be so long. Soon the first place will be theirs. And it will be so the sooner, the more faithful they are in their preparation for it. Into all the various questions that disturb the surface, or even reach into the depths of social life, we may bring the fresh enthusiasm of youth, and decide them by the infusion into them of a better spirit. The old prejudices, the ancient wrongs, that even now seek to perpetuate themselves at the cost of all things dear to human welfare, may receive their death-blow at the hands of the true and earnest men of to-day, who join, with the strength of youth, the wisdom of righteous principle and the courage of a noble soul!

We should not, it is true, forget our indebtedness to the past for much of what we now have and enjoy. It is because of the faithful labors, the victorious struggles, the willing sacrifices, and the heroic self-devotion of men in the past, that we rejoice to-day in the secure possession of our manifold benefits. It is because, in the great exigencies of the past, when truth and righteousness, justice and liberty, trembled on the verge of defeat, there have been men who loved truth and righteousness, justice and liberty, better than their own advantage and their own lives, that the triumph was gained, and that we enjoy the fruits of the victory. Other men have labored, and we are always entering into their labors. They have sowed the seed, and we gather in the harvest, now whitening all the fields. We can not look upon the lives of those good and true men who have gone before us with disrespect, without losing a portion of the best part of ourselves. The reverence for nobleness which has been exhibited in any man's life, is a grand incitement to nobleness in one's own life.

And this, indeed, is the spirit with which young men should look back to the past; not to perpetuate its evil and wrong; still less to seek apologies for inaction and indifference toward the good and right; but, rather and always to feel inspired to better and nobler lives in the present, than any that have yet been lived. We should not look back upon those ages, which we call sacred, as though they never could be repeated, but try to understand and thoroughly believe that we can make our own age sacred. It is not the time, in history, but the men of history, that make the time heroic, and in all ages duty has been the real basis of heroism. And we ourselves, to-day, having the same nature, heart, conscience, soul, that have lived in man in the best age of history, may make the present as full of real nobility as the past, add our contribution to the sum of human welfare, and our names to the honored list of the world's true men.

There is a kind of conservatism which is timid and fearful; which looks backward instead of forward; which has no hope and no cheerful faith. It refuses to engage in the movements of the times, because they are revolutionary. It is content to let the world go on its way, and raises no hand to help its necessities; for why should the existing order be disturbed? It is tenacious of all things old, and would touch no prevailing wrong, if it have the sanction of antiquity. It excuses every evil that curses the race, because it has existed; and, in the midst of its ancestral comfort, pride and place, it refuses to reach down to the struggling, perishing classes of men below it, or give them the aid and sympathy which they require. Like Old Mortality, it gropes about among the tombs of a buried past, to renew their useless inscriptions, and re-build the monuments of men whom the world would be very glad to forget.

Such is not the conservatism which should dwell in a young man's life. He should look back upon the past to be incited by the noble examples which it furnishes; to have his love of liberty fired by the remembrance of the martyrs to the cause of the world's freedom; to have duty made more honorable by its connection with all the honored sons of men; to have the flame of religion kindled by contact with the divine fire that burns upon the world's altars of devotion! He should desire to preserve and enlarge the good which the past has wrought; while the whole energy of his nature should be employed in diminishing and putting an end to the evil which the past has left. He should be bold, laying hold upon life with a firm, strong hand. He should be courageous, throwing himself into the breach, where assaulting parties march on to victory over the beleaguered wrong of centuries. He should take counsel of his hopes and not of his fears, and press forward to the triumph which awaits all right endeavor. Or, if failure comes, it will be a failure which loses every sting of defeat by reason of the courage with which and the noble end for which the battle has been waged. This is the young man's true conservatism — not of falsehood, though it be ever so respectable — but of all genuine righteousness and all truthful honor!

The present has its responsibilities, which it is always laying upon young men. If we are indebted to the past for any good, we are responsible to the present for its right use. Here and now are duties to be done, which can not possibly be neglected with safety. They come up to us from all the places of human life, demanding of us a faithful attention and a faithful work. The time which is allowed any of us must of necessity be short, even at the longest. So much the more imperative become the duties of the time. It is not to be wasted. It is not to be squandered in useless extravagance, nor dissipated in destructive pleasures. It is not to be abused in petty tyranny over the weak, nor is it to be lost in servile sycophancy before the strong. It is not to be allowed to run away in shallow streams, affording no fruitful resource, or in idle pursuits, accomplishing no worthy object. It is to be used for good results and worthy ends. It is to be preserved from every moth and rust. It is to be filled with the best and truest deeds. It is to be like the deep and mighty river, bearing the wealth of states upon its surface, and, in the bosom of its waters, the fertilizing influence which covers all the fields along its course with plenty, and fills a continent with blessing! And, over all, shall be the smiling heavens, bright with the benedictions of God!

There are obligations to the future as well as responsibilities to the present and indebtedness to the past. No man takes a wise, judicious, or even proper view of life, who does not include in it a prospect of the future. He must take into the account the consequences of his actions, as well as the actions themselves. He must understand that he is under the great law of cause and effect, and that what he does to-day will have the widest results in all the days to come. It is not simply that the days of early life are passing over him with their sweet, bright influence. It is not simply that life is all fresh and new, and the sun is bright, and the sky has no cloud. It is, that there are other days and other years, flowing out of these; that the time is coming when the face of the sky will be clouded over, and the sun will be darkened. It is well that these bright days should pass with such trusty faithfulness, that they shall leave behind, in memory, nothing to make the dark days darker; every thing which shall send rays of blessed sunshine into the cloudy years that are before us. We may, even now, store away in our souls such precious and bright possessions, as will enrich our lives through their whole course — as shall strengthen us in all time to come. He who works for the future in the present hour, is working well. He who knows that every faithful work in the present is a work for the future, has a wise understanding of life. The engineer builds a bridge, not simply to span a placid, Summer stream, but strong enough to withstand the greatest force of the Spring-time freshet. Every stone which he lays, in raising the massive piers, is laid for the future exigency, and the greater his faithfulness in the present work, the more secure will be the structure for its future needs. The ultimate and the final are kept in view equally with the immediate and original. Let the young man so live and work in the present, as not to be ashamed of what he has done, when, by and by, he looks back upon his accomplishment. Sad enough will it be, if he shall add to the weakness of his future years the shame of conscious neglect and unworthiness in the present days, and if, in the midst of the ruins of his manhood, he shall weep over the unrepented follies and sins of a misspent youth.

The demand thus made upon young men is, in the highest sense, connected with all goodness and greatness of character. All that the past furnishes, all that the present possesses, and all that the future may have in it, unite in calling upon the young man of our times to be faithful to what he already has, and to what may, by diligence, obtain. This appeal is made, not that he may add to his outward acquirements, so much as to those accomplishments of character, which will make him truly wise and truly wealthy; that he may augment the worth of his manhood, more than the value of his property, and that he may become more manly, honest and true, as he grows in years. There is no one of us so poor as to be deprived of real enjoyment in the use of his mental and spiritual faculties, or to suffer destitution of the best things of life. We all are rich in the possession of the noblest examples. We all may run our course of life parallel with the worthiest of our race. The possibilities of our manhood are of the highest kind, and there is no attainment of personal excellence that we should allow ourselves to dispair of. We must not disappoint the future of its expected triumphs. We must not allow any thing good to be lost by our indifference, or selfishness, or neglect, but go forward with unwearied step, fulfilling the promise which we have given, and more than meeting the expectation which the age awaits. We can if we will. If we will not, we are faithless to our trust.

I think, too, we owe something to the land in which we live, and to the glories of its history. We ought to change the meaning of that term, given us too often as a reproach, and make our "Young American" manhood the type of all that is noble and worthy of ourselves and our origin. We have too long suffered under the opprobrium which the vices and indulgences, the dishonesty and crime, the recklessness and bravado, the rioting and debauchery of many of our young men have brought upon the American character. We ought not to allow ourselves to suffer under the contempt of the world, because our young men go abroad, and, neglecting the highest and best things of the old civilization, return with the worst part of European customs; because we repudiate the payment of our debts, and fail of meeting our engagements; because we pour out hordes of piratical adventurers to steal a weaker neighbor's property; because we palliate the existence of the worst oppression, in the midst of our boasts of republicanism and democracy. It belongs to us, in part, my brothers, to put a new meaning to the phrase, "Young America;" to make it expressive of all that is true, just, honest, honorable and manly; to give the world assurance that this new continent rears a nation of free men, who are distinguished for all the virtues of a Christian civilization. Let us cast off our reproach, and be true to the great ideas of our national life — that the fathers of our republic may not have lived in vain, or that we ourselves may not subsist upon the honor of a noble ancestry. Let us make it abundantly manifest that we are living, not wholly for trade and dishonest speculation, and the exercise of power over the weak, and the accumulations of our gains at the expense of others; but for all graceful yet manly culture, for all upright and generous enterprise, for all noble and heroic adventure, for all eminence in true national greatness, crowning the whole with a genuine religion! This must be most especially true as it regards us of New-England, who have so bright a record in the past and such hopes of glory in the future. Here would we work for truth, and liberty, and God!

"It concerneth New-England men always to remember," said the celebrated Higginson, in 1663, "that they are a plantation religious, and not a plantation of trade. Let merchants, and such others as are increasing cent. per cent., remember this, that worldly gain was not the end and design of the people of New-England, but religion. And if any man among us make religion as twelve and the world as thirteen, such an one has not the spirit of a true New-England man."

Have we the ability thus to work? There are certain qualities of character, as it were, natural to young men, which, if rightly directed, are capable of accomplishing all this and more. Let me briefly recount them:

1. Freshness. The young man brings to the work of life a fresh strength. His opinions are newly formed. He is not affected by prejudice. He is not bound by the fetters of custom and convention. The subjects which appeal to his attention, and ask for discussion, come to him as new subjects, without the influence of old associations. Unhampered by precedent, independent in thought, and free in mind, he approaches his task, and if it is not readily accomplished, his endeavors in it are worthy of all commendation. It is a great advantage to have this fresh element of youth continually pouring in upon the movements of human thought. It is like the breath of Spring upon the cold Winter of the year. It is like the pure breezes of the open country upon the close and deadened atmosphere of the crowded city. Old men sometimes smile, and perhaps oftener rebuke the extravagance of young men's opinions. But it is a healthy extravagance, if it is honestly held, and it serves to prevent that stagnation of thought which is most of all to be dreaded. It is a good thing to have the discussion and the work of life freshened by our young men!

2*

2. GENEROSITY. A young man is usually generous in his estimate of life. He looks out upon the world with a wide view. He is free from the narrowness which the selfish policy of subsequent years produces; and, in the high spirit of generous resolution, he goes forth to the duty before him. This generosity of character may be perverted and abused; yet, in its true exercise, it is an admirable quality. We are glad that it is characteristic of youth. Selfishness comes on speedily enough at the latest, and it is fortunate for us that there is one season of life comparatively free from its destructive presence; when the soul looks out with healthy and generous eyes upon the objects around it; is willing to believe and trust; rejoices in the liberal thought of life, and is grateful for the promise which it makes!

3. ENTHUSIASM. Young men are generally full of this feeling. Nothing seems to be difficult. Every thing is easy. The way is clear before the mind. The obstructions and hindrances are not perceived, or, if regarded at all, are deemed of slight importance. For with all this generous power of heart, and mind, and soul, there can hardly be a doubt of success. Indeed, enthusiasm is always requisite for success. We have little faith in a cool, calculating, indifferent man, who is never astonished at any thing, however wonderful; who is more disposed to reason than to act, and who receives every proposition with a doubting hesitancy, and by his excessive caution loses the opportunity of

striking the decisive blow at the decisive time. We know how such men as these throw a dampening and chilling influence over every worthy enterprise, and freeze it into complete inertion. We dread to meet such men. How much better and more encouraging to meet a man who inspires our own enthusiasm by his cheering coöperation and his ready confidence!

"There is," says Bacon, "surely no greater wisdom than well to time the beginning and onset of things. Dangers are no more light, if they once seem light. It were better to meet some dangers half way, than to keep too long a watch upon their approaches. The ripeness and unripeness of the occasion must ever be well weighed; and generally it is good to commit the beginnings of all great actions to Argus, with his hundred eyes, and to Briareus, with his hundred arms—first to watch and then to speed. There is no seeing comparable to celerity—like the motion of a bullet in the air, which flieth so swift as it outruns the eye."

4. Hope. This belongs to the early part of life in an eminent degree. The young man has no retrospect. It is all prospect. He has nothing to do but to look forward; and in that forward view he sees every thing pertaining to a successful life. He rarely thinks of disappointment. It seldom enters into his calculations. There are no clouds. It is all sunshine, happiness and joy; and he hastens forward, never doubting that the prize which he seeks will speedily be in his grasp, and the mark at which he aims com-

pletely attained. Soon, he meets with defeat and disappointment. But his hope is still strong that every loss will be retrieved and the victory will be gained at last. Is not this better than to sit down weakened and despairing, and refuse to labor, supposing it useless? No true man is he, who allows a single failure or defeat to overcome his purpose. It is cowardly to fall prostrate before misfortune. It is unmanly, and more cowardly still to seek an escape from trouble by an escape from life. It is more manly, brave and true, to live through and over misfortune, and in the most disheartening circumstances, "never say, die!"

5. Energy. The young man joins, with all the other qualities of character, a prompt energy. He takes hold with an energetic grasp. He goes to his work with a will. So general is this characteristic, that it is an exception and a matter of remark to find a young man who prefers indolence to exertion, and is more willing to waste his time in utter idleness, than to improve it by active energy. We look upon him, not only as a man who forfeits our respect, but as one who is untrue to his own nature and the best qualities of his character. It is not in accordance with our feelings or our thoughts respecting the true worth of young manhood, to see idleness preferred to useful work, and the best part of life misused in folly and indulgence, preparing for a manhood of bitter regrets and an old age of sorrowful memories! "The glory of young men is their strength," says the Hebrew moralist. But when

that glory has been changed into shame, by their own folly, it is a sad thing for the whole life. Such clouds as this will bring are not cleared away. They settle down in darkness over the life forever.

We can not shut our eyes to the fact that there is a well grounded apprehension that these qualities of character may be perverted and abused. To escape this danger, to make it certain that they shall be used as they ought, it is needful that they should be consecrated to right and truth, by a spirit of loyalty to religious principle. There is no danger to a young man, with all his restless activity, if he can keep himself true to his own convictions of duty. The natural qualities of character which he possesses, are the most effective for accomplishing the best results for himself and for all the race. He can, if he will, make the whole world debtor to him. He can, if he will, grow a manhood which shall be the reality of beauty and nobility, such as the world has never witnessed. When we look upon the noblest works of art, the almost breathing marble, the almost speaking canvas, we are stirred with emotions of admiration. Our own souls are moved to action. We, too, would wish to possess and use the genius which has planned, the skill which has produced the sculpture or painting that attracts our gaze. Ah! believe me, we are engaged upon a work far transcending any such production, great though it be. We are engaged in carving out a sculpture more enduring than marble. We are engaged in depicting what shall be bright and fresh when the colors of the artist have faded, and the canvas has crumbled — a nobler work than the genius of sculptor or painter has yet devised!

Let us, then, be faithful to what we have inherited from the past, faithful to the duties which the present hour brings, faithful to the expectations which the future waits for; faithful to the age in which we live, and the land we are proud and glad to call our own! Let our fresh vigor be kept unstained and unpolluted. If there is an object most to be pitied, it is that of a young man who professes to be sick and tired of life; who finds nothing around him to awaken his ambition, or call out his energies, and passes his days in listlessness and sloth. Let him arouse himself to the work of life, and be true to his own soul and its necessities of exertion! Let our generosity pour out its treasures for the benefit of the world. That is the truest life which lives for others' good. Let it be as the Divine and Christly generosity, which continually flows out upon mankind in true benevolence and unselfish charity. Let our enthusiasm be employed to the furtherance of the highest and purest ends. In the old language of the past, enthusiasm meant the inspiration of the gods. So, in our day, the enthusiasm of youth may be like the inspired presence of a Deity — filled with a divine purpose, and acting upon all human life with an almost divine power.

Finally, let hope and energy have their consecration

to the prosecution of the worthiest enterprises. It is a grand sight, that of a man pursuing some great plan with an enthusiasm that is never quenched, with a hope that never falters, and an energy that is never wearied; like Columbus, seeking a new world — like Newton, searching the depths of space for the wonders of the universe — like Wilberforce, freeing whole tribes of men from cruel servitude — like Luther, leading out the faculties of the mind from a bondage worse than Egyptian slavery. We, too, have a great plan to follow — a great end to secure. Let us, too, with enthusiastic energy and with buoyant hope, live and work for liberty and truth. There are triumphs yet to be achieved by all true and earnest men. Heaven's roll is never full of the names of the just. Let our names, too, be written on that eternal record, which bears the story of immortal virtue!

"I know that age to age succeeds,
Blowing a noise of tongues and deeds,
A dust of systems and of creeds.

"I can not hide that some have striven,
Achieving calm, to whom is given
The joy that mixes man with Heaven:

"Who, rowing hard against the stream,
Saw distant gates of Eden gleam,
And did not dream it was a dream;

"But heard, by secret transport led,
Even in the charnels of the dead,
The murmur of the fountain-head —

"Which did accomplish their desire,
Bore and forebore, and did not tire;
Like Stephen an unquenched fire.

"He heeded not reviling tones,
Nor sold his heart to idle moans,
Though cursed and scorned and bruised with stones:

"But, looking upward, full of grace,
He prayed, and from a happy place,
God's glory smote him on the face."

II. THE YOUNG MAN AT HOME.

In my last Lecture I spoke sufficiently of the young man's duties to himself to prepare him for the work of a man in the present age. We saw him to be rich in the examples of nobleness which the past has furnished—earnest in his fidelity to the present and the future, and consecrating the fresh energy, enthusiasm, vigor and hope of his early days to the purest and highest purposes. By such means he becomes capable of accomplishing the best and most glorious results.

But there are relations to others which demand consideration. As no man liveth, and no man can live to himself alone—as his own happiness and good must depend, in a great measure, upon those around him, and theirs, too, reciprocally, upon him—it becomes a matter of considerable importance to understand how best the relations to others can be improved for the good of the whole.

First in time, if not the first in rank, come forward the duties which the young man owes at home — to his family and kindred. So I have decided to ask your attention this evening to a consideration of the Domestic Duties of Young Men.

Those of you who have been constant attendants upon the weekly service in this place, know that our thoughts have frequently been directed to the contemplation of home duties, because, I have no doubt in my own mind, the institution of the family has, under Providence, a vast influence, not only upon individual character, but also upon the progress of civilization and religion. Had we time to devote to it, the power of home and its influence upon the character of the human race, would be a subject well worthy our investigation. I think it can be shown that those nations have the truest theory of civilization, and the truest practice, also, which have the most regard to home and its duties, and among which home holds a high and sacred place. We, of the Anglo Saxon race, are accustomed to think of ourselves as standing in the van; as holding the front rank in the onward march of mankind. It is not without reason that we are accustomed thus to think. There can be no question that in energy, in perseverance, in skill in the useful arts, in ideas of government and theories of religion, we do stand in the front rank. Let us once understand what can be done by man, and there will always be found enough among us willing and able to do it. And it will not be difficult to determine how much of all this is due to the influence of home; for home is peculiarly an Anglo Saxon word, with a peculiar Anglo Saxon meaning. Just so it is. With us, home is the grand though quiet theater of our noblest and purest duties, and in its true character becomes to us not only an educating influence, exerted upon one's own manhood, but also the educating influence of society. It has been called, and not unjustly, the conscience of society; for it certainly is the regulating principle of social forces. It is but necessary that there should be a right home education to produce a state of society which would be, so far as possible, perfect. So convinced am I of this fact, that there is nothing which I would wish to guard with more sacred and constant vigilance than the home affections; nothing which I would oppose with a more strenuous resistance than that which in any way attacks, or undervalues, or seeks to undermine them. All social evils find their worst result in the destruction of these; in the rupture of domestic ties; in the overthrow of that institution of the family, on which, as a foundation, the fabric of society rests most securely. What gives intemperance such a dreadful character is, in most part, that it degrades and destroys home. What is one of the worst features of Slavery is, that it separates families, makes the marriage tie depend simply upon custom, and caprice, and ownership, and stains the holiest affections of human nature with a vile concupiscence. What seems to me the most dangerous as well as the most revolting aspect of Mormonism is, not the slavish subjection of the mind to a priestly domination — for that is a characteristic of other communities; — but the sanctioned practice of polygamy debasing, uncivilized, and fatal as it must be to all the best interests of human life.

It is true, that this feeling respecting home may degenerate into a selfish love of home comforts and ease; and that it may so completely engross the heart as to shut out the recollection of those who are homeless. One may be so fully occupied with his own home as to forget the claims of those outside of its walls, and be unmindful of his duties toward them. But that is by no means a legitimate result. A right home education always takes into account that the pure and warm affections which expand amid the quickening influences of domestic life, are not narrow or exclusive in their embrace. One soon learns that under the truth of what Jesus has taught respecting God and man, all mankind form one great family, and that it is none other than a brother or a sister whom we are called upon to love and labor for. One soon learns that the ties of kindred connect all human life together, and, as they extend, invisibly, but every where, throughout the world of human effort and human labor, join us all in one grand unity, to promote and strengthen which is the great object of our earthly existence.

I think, then, I do not over-estimate the domestic duties of young men when I bring forward their consideration as of prime importance. Is it necessary that I should urge you to love your homes? That love is even now in all our hearts. We can not wholly eradicate, indeed we would not wish to do it, the love we feel for the home we have quitted; nor can we break the ties which bind us to it. It belongs to the human heart to cast a retrospective eye upon the scenes of early life, and recall again the affections which were its first blessing. When a man goes out, in early life, from the home which sheltered him, to contend, as best he may, with the world about him, he may burrow in the golden mine, he may plunge into the heart of the primeval forest, he may trust his fortune upon the treacherous ocean, or mingle in the strife of the city's busy crowds, but still, in every lull of the boisterous elements of his life, there come stealing in upon him thoughts of home and early days. The scenes through which he wandered in childhood's heedless innocence, or boyhood's daring play — the old school-house, which had witnessed his first attempts to find his way to knowledge — the sunny hill-side and the plain, on whose soft carpet of springing grass he had spent many an hour of careless enjoyment — the wild flowers that grew upon the banks of the murmuring brook — the woods and the rocky rills — all are there upon the memory; no one faded, and none lost. And in the center stands the dear old homestead — some low-browed cottage, under the hill or on the river bank, or by the shore of the sea, or some ancestral mansion, with its family histories to make it venerable. And as he thinks of all this, in delightful reverie, he seems to feel once more around him the father's strong arm, and hear once more his words of manly counsel; a mother's tear wets his cheek, and her gentle kiss is felt upon his lips! The needle of his being may have many variations, as it becomes subjected to various influences;

yet it is still true to one place, and that place is where he spent his early days, or where his fathers dwelt. Almost imperceptibly to himself, he is filled with longing for a return to these scenes whose memory has so lightened his toils. The successful business man looks forward to the time when he can lay aside his cares, and go quietly home to rest. The soldier, amid war's alarms, dreams, in the nightly bivouacs of his distant campaigns, of

> "The pleasant fields traversed so oft,
> In life's morning march, when his bosom was young!"

The professional man would retire from the exhausting labors of his work, and, closing peacefully a life of graceful culture, pass the evening of his days in literary leisure, among the scenes where his first lessons had been learned. The statesman wearies of the strifes of party and the forum, and the applause of the senate house, and sighs for some quiet retreat among the old friends and neighbors that have watched his aspiring career, and felt an honest pride in his triumphs. And those who are compelled to spend their whole lives away from home, and can not hope to return, still desire that at the last their dust will mingle with the ashes of their fathers, in the old churchyard which contains the mortal part of those whom they have once known and loved.

> "Fresh as the first beam glittering on a sail,
> That brings our friends up from the under world,

Sad as the last, which reddens over one,
That sinks, with all we love, below the verge:
So sad, so fresh the days that are no more!"

Believe me, these remembrances are to all of us a saving power in this heated and exciting city life — a saving power—for the thought, that your wrong and sin will not spend the force of its blow till it has reached and shattered those hearts at home which are always turned toward you, and are most tenderly sensible of every thing you are now and here doing, will be a restraint between you and the wickedness you would commit, and will stay the hand which is lifted to do a deed of sin. It will become a strengthening power, too, for the remembrance of the fact that there are others watching your course with anxious and loving solicitude, and whose life you will make brighter and more joyful by your fidelity, will impel you to be faithful, both to your own manhood and their fond expectations. Never, then, my friend, allow your love of home to be weakened or in any way lessened. Cherish it as among the best affections, and as among those powers which are the choicest treasures of your manhood. It is a power and it is a treasure which will most essentially weaken and impoverish you to lose.

It is a sad thing for a man when the influences and recollections of early life cease to have power over him. It is a sad thing for a man when he becomes ashamed of them; when, in the midst of school, or college, or business life, he allows himself to forget his early days and the friends who have cherished him. It is a terrible thing for those who love him to trace the marks which sensuality and dissipation make upon the features that they have loved to look upon, and to see how the freshness and purity of home life is lost under the brutalizing influence of self-indulgence and vice. No! we can not afford to lose the remembrances of early days, and the power of home affections!

For the sake of greater directness and clearness, let me be a little more particular and specific. To speak in general terms of domestic duties, does not appear to me sufficiently explicit; and so I divide the subject into its appropriate heads.

1. Of course the most obvious and the first must be the filial duties of young men — those which are owed to parents. A good son — one who remembers that parents expect much from his fidelity, and who is anxious not to disappoint the expectation; who remembers that the joy of those who reared him in infancy, is now dependent upon him, and who wishes to be their support and solace in the years of weakness; who feels that obedience and respect and honor are not only their due, but his imperative obligation, and whose great business it is to be obedient and respectful, is almost morally certain of being a good and honorable and upright man. And this duty of his is one of gratitude. For who was it that watched over your infancy with such a tender care; who helped your helplessness, who strengthened your weakness, and

guarded your earliest years with such a watchful vigilance? Who was the best and most faithful counselor of your youth and early manhood, with that disinterested friendship and love which only a parent can feel? Who but the father, whose manly love was given in its fullness for your good? Who but the mother, in whose heart of hearts there was always a choice place reserved for you; who first forgave your faults; who first encouraged you to faithfulness; of whose love, in all your wanderings and errors, you are most sure, and whose approbation of your success is always most welcome? Is it possible that all this can be forgotten, and that the young man in his folly should turn away from the recollection or the counsels of those friends who have always been true and most constant, to hearken to the solicitations and listen to the allurements of those whose best professions of friendship are a falsehood? It is not simply empty protestations of regard and esteem, which a man should make in return for the fullness of parental love which is poured on him. Words are but very little and very weak. They who are most really contentious in families are generally those who are most profuse in words of affection. But it is the act of fidelity to right convictions. It is not even the fear of parents' displeasure that should be the restraint from the contemplated sin, nor the expectation of parental approval, that should be the encouragement to virtue. But it is the reflection that a course of wrong will be for a parent's unspeakable grief and pain; that a course of right and truthfulness for a parent's unspeakable happiness and joy. It is the remembrance that your failure injures not yourself alone, but will also bring gray hairs in sorrow to the grave; that your success will not only give you joy, but will make the burden of years lighter, and give a quicker buoyancy to all the life of those at home. There is not a parent within the hearing of my voice to-night but is proud of a faithful son — but is ashamed and sad for a foolish and unfaithful one. And is it not sufficient for you, young men, to understand this as most unquestionably true in the case of your own parents? I trust that there is no one of us who does not appreciate the value of genuine parental love; which spends itself and knows no weariness for the good of those dependent upon its power. Life is more full of joy for all its influence of good. He that has a parent's life to look upon, which has been always faithful and true, has something rich and full, which he can not be deprived of without great injury. It is a blessing from heaven that such a life is given him. How beautifully Tennyson describes a mother! One

> Not learned, save in gracious household ways;
> Not perfect, nay, but full of tender wants;
> No angel, but a dearer being, all dipt
> In angel instincts, breathing Paradise, —
> Interpreter between the gods and men.
> Who looked all native to her place, and yet

On tiptoe seemed to touch upon a sphere
Too gross to tread, and all male minds perforce
Swayed to her from their orbits as they moved,
And girdled her with music. Happy he
With such a mother! Trust in all things high
Comes easy to him, and though he trip and fall,
He shall not blind his soul with clay.

It may be that there are exceptions to all this. There may be unfaithfulness in parents. Their duties may not be performed as they should be. But even where this is the case, the obligation is not wholly wanting. For it may be the means, if it is truly met, of exercising a beneficial influence upon the parent's life, and even the means, as it has been in some instances, of its salvation. I do not see, then, any way in which filial duties can be avoided; and I know of nothing nobler or more beautiful than the fidelity to such duties — where the manliness of opening life furnishes a support for the declining vigor of old age; where the debt of early years is repaid with grateful constancy; where tottering steps are guided with tenderness, and weakening years are strengthened with ready help; where a successful and useful life is made more honorable by the knowledge that its success and usefulness will make the heart of age rejoice, and send the blood with quicker flow through all its sluggish course.

2. Brotherly duties, there are — to gladden a sister's life, to aid in unfolding a brother's character.

There can be no doubt that brothers' influence upon each other and upon sisters is of the strongest kind. It is a singular tie, this of family relationship, and the influence that is exercised upon its connections is of a wonderful nature. It is a mysterious union, and one having most momentous consequences. Between brothers and sisters there is generally more confidence than between parents and children; and the reason is obvious. A nearer equality of age, a freer intercourse, a unity of pursuits, all conduce to less restraint and more open deportment toward each other. Where there are, as there should be, a regard always for each other's happiness and welfare, a constant remembrance of the claims of each upon the other, and a fidelity in answering those claims; where the intercourse is always of the most kindly sort, there can be no question of its excellent influence in shaping the character and increasing the good of all. Most especially is this true of an elder brother. And where, as happens not seldom, the head of the family may be removed by death, and a widowed mother leans upon him for support, and younger brothers and sisters look up to him for example, while the responsibility is increased, the means of good are likewise increased. The elder brother then becomes, as he deserves to be, the most important, as he is the most privileged member of the household circle. We all understand that there is nothing more conducive to one's happiness in after life, and not only that, but also to his real good and usefulness, than a happy home with its excellent educating influences. We all ought to understand that in producing that happiness and promoting that good, each one has his or her part to do. The art of living happily with others may be a very difficult one to acquire, but it is so, because there is a forgetfulness on the part of the different persons, that each one has somewhat of happiness and good to contribute as well as to receive, and that each one should see that the contribution is always generously made. Every one indeed has very much to learn—how mutual forbearance—a control of temper—self-forgetfulness—and a true love for others' good, are the means of filling one's home with happiness—and I know of none who can teach it better by a continual example, than a generous, true, manly elder brother.

3. The time comes to every one, when the affections pass beyond the home walls—when the love of brother and sister, of father and mother, does not satisfy—and the heart must find some one who shall be dearer to it than all others. Here I am aware that we are coming to exceedingly delicate ground, and it is with careful step that we must pursue our way. In affairs of the heart, no one can give advice. Yet a few suggestions may not be altogether out of place. Indeed, so far as these matters are concerned, I am confident that no subject becomes more worthy the young man's attention, involving as it does, oftentimes, the whole happiness of his after life—and not his own happiness

alone, but that of another whose welfare should be nearest his heart. So, too, there are dangers which environ this time of life, which demand a word of caution—dangers lest passion should be master and not a real affection—lest love should degenerate into lust—lest a too hasty preference, founded on no substantial qualities of mind or heart, should take the place of a profound regard which only grows deeper and stronger as the years of married life move on. There are too many ill-conditioned and wrongly advised marriages now embittering human life to allow me to pass over a matter fraught with such consequences of joy or sorrow, in silence or without heed. God has so created us, that a union of the sexes is almost a necessity of our nature for its proper development, and there is no question that when that union takes place under the influence of a genuine mutual affection, the best and happiest results to one's self and all human life will be its issue. The best and gentlest part of our nature becomes developed and becomes active. The most beautifying graces of character blossom out even from the rudest natures. Over the life spreads a new glory and brightness. Love, of which poets have sung, and which every true man and woman feels, at some time in his or her life, with a thrill of heart and soul, which shows that human nature is not all lost in the depths of a sinful selfishness—is indeed not alone the master spirit of life, but is also the good genius of life. He who gives it free and generous scope, and keeps it pure and warm within him, gives himself nobility. He who debases it into a wicked passion, and makes himself its victim, is doing himself immeasurable wrong—is losing his best possession, and is abusing one of the divinest gifts ever bestowed upon man by the mercy of the Father. Of what blessed and blissful humanities has true love been the source! What scorching flames, devouring with insatiate greed body, mind and soul, have been kindled by a shameless lust!

So I would ask you not to abuse this blessing of your life. But I fear it is abused in various ways. One too common way is that mischievous, thoughtless, and heartless conduct, which, in the language of the day, is called flirtation. A female coquette is indeed contemptible, but a male flirt is far more so. The man who, in his careless selfishness will give himself, perhaps in amusement or from caprice, to trifling with the best affections of another—and that other a woman—who will refuse in his willfulness to understand how much pain and sorrow, perhaps for a lifetime he is causing—who is ever seeking in his foolish dalliance for some new companion to please his fancy—false and faithless as he is—is despicable and worthless. Let no young man who hears me ever put himself into such a position. While it is one of dishonor to himself, it is one of misery to others, and the thought of that, at least, should operate as a restraint. True, indeed, there is much foolish sentimentalism in this matter—which it is not for me to indulge in—but aside from that, it is a matter of exceeding seriousness, which we should all do well to heed.

Out of it too often grows that character — the worst embodiment of human wickedness — the avowed and acknowledged libertine. The language does not furnish terms for expressing the just abhorrence of him, whose cruel desires are never satisfied—whose life is one continued sin — whose systematic course is that of ruin to himself and others — who plays with the unsuspecting victims of his wiles with utter heartlessness—and leaves them at last to a bitter and wretched destruction. There is many a course of shame, and of shamelessness—of that peculiar crime of great cities—which had its beginning in the first destruction of womanly innocence and purity at the hands of the seducer. I am not blind to the fact that there are persons of this class belonging to both sexes; but even when this is so, it is because the honor and virtue of the woman have been first destroyed by man. The general opinion of society is in part censurable for this. For while the woman finds herself devoid of sympathy, even from her own sex, and is shut out from the use of the means of reformation, the man who has done all the mischief still retains his social position, is as much caressed and smiled on as before, finds himself no less respectable, and, though every step he takes mercilessly crushes hearts that have been too confiding, there is no one to shudder at his baseness—

no one to deny him friendship. Till but very lately, there was no law in all the land by which he could be punished for his crime. We have yet to learn pity and compassion for the tempted one; we have yet to learn abhorrence of the tempter—that there is no punishment too severe for him—no word too expressive to declare his guilt! Do not abuse, young man, oh do not abuse this blessing of the Father's love; this mysterious power of attraction which draws human hearts toward each other, that each may find its complement and enjoy its full satisfaction of affection.

4. Avoiding these dangers then, when the time comes for building up a new home, let its foundations be laid in that true affection which is the blessing of life—in that mutual confidence and high regard which can alone insure happiness—in that spirit of religion, of dependence upon God, of piety and trust, which throws its beauty round about the household, and spreads over it a glory which is born of Heaven itself. Marriage is a Divine institution, full of good to man. It is full of responsibility too, and of duty—never to be entered except with a profound understanding of what there is of duty and of good in it—never in heedlessness and thoughtlessness and haste. If entered upon aright, there is no question that married life, consecrated by the spirit of religion and pursued with mutual forbearance, has a fullness of happiness and good in all its course. It is a discipline, too, of man's nobler powers, and of his highest virtues. There

are consequences of the most important moment to individual happiness and good, and to social welfare in the habitual intercourse of men and women with each other. It is not safe, even in the smallest degree, to blunt the keenest edge, or dim the finest temper of principle. There can be no such thing as security in trifling with the most sacred obligations of life. There is great danger that youthful purity will become corrupted, and that which should be the crown of virtue in woman and honor in man be made a by-word and reproach! No one can thus live with a constant feeling that there is another depending upon him for support, for protection, for welfare; no one can live with a surety of help given him in all his hours of weariness, of encouragement in the enterprise of his life, of rest after his conflicts with the world, of safe and secure refuge within home walls from the ills of outside life, where the noise and din and toil of life may be shut out, and peace shall dwell forever, without being a better and more manly man, in every way. His manhood grows into larger and fuller proportions. And, if to the duties of a husband are added the duties of a parent, and the young man finds a new life given him to tend and care for and unfold into beauty and power, the added responsibility gives a new meaning and importance to his life. So the home duties of the young man culminate in these. These are the highest to which he will be called. Here, too, he must share the labor of education and training with the mother and the wife. He can not afford to give to his business what belongs to his children. To become the head of a family of his own — to watch over lives with the anxiety and affection by which his own early years were attended — to aid in the formation of a character moulding for eternal results—to help the growth of an immortal soul ripening for the everlasting fruitage of heaven — to walk the way of life so faithfully and so carefully that those who look to him for an example to copy shall not wander from the right — to bring out and forward before God and man a noble manhood from amid the circumstances of life, that so the generation coming on shall take pattern by it and produce a nobler still — all this is a work for the young man to do; and if faithfully done, it shall be for the benefit of many generations. There is a new solemnity and dignity given to one's life by the knowledge of duties of such a character. One can not but be taken out of much that is mean and small and trifling, and made to feel that there is more in human life than he had ever dreamed of — that his own life has a higher character, because others' lives are bound up with it for their weal or woe. So we would accept all these various things as sacred trusts given to our hands and hearts by Providence. So we would try to be faithful to them, making good returns for what we have received by an unfailing and rightful use of powers and privileges, and so doing our duties to our fellow-men by constancy at home.

I think it is a mistake to suppose that upon the wife falls all the responsibility of making home what it should be. It belongs to the husband as well. He is apt to think that when he has been absent through the day, diligent in his work and harassed by the cares of business, his duty is done. He expects a ready and loving smile to welcome him, a warm and cordial greeting — and he should have it. But he must remember that the wife has had her cares too. If of a different character, they may be equally harassing. The wife has had her labor to perform as well, and when the night comes, she may be as weary too. Does she not deserve as much consideration and kindness? No toils of business and no cares of life should be allowed to come in to prevent that kind and grateful intercourse which makes up the good of life. The burden should be equally borne. The joy should be shared together, and the quiet rest of domestic life should belong to both alike.

If all these matters are as I have declared them to be, I think I have by no means erred in urging them upon your attention at this early stage of our considerations. And so I conclude as I commenced by pressing upon your minds and hearts the obligation of fidelity to home — its various lessons and its various duties. They are at the bottom of all true success in life; they are the soul of all social blessing; they are the spirit of all true patriotism. Good homes make good communities. And the influences that go out from good homes build up a noble, manly people into a nationality, which shall be strong and enduring, filled with justice and freedom, righteousness and truth. It is fortunate for us, friends, that we have in our Anglo Saxon speech the word — that in our Anglo Saxon hearts we love it, with a love never to be broken. Ah! let the power in the heart be a power on the tongue, and in the hand, to stop every word and deed of anger and strife; to make all our life a practical obedience to one great lesson, the helping of each other in our lifetime's work; to fit us for usefulness and make us grow in manliness abroad; to help us to fidelity to society; that we strive in our feeble way, satisfied, however, that no good effort of ours is ever lost, to solve those social problems that so vex men's minds, and do our part toward destroying those that cause so much misery and wretchedness; to help us to fidelity to the state, to love liberty, to hate oppression, to abhor injustice, to raise here a national structure, which shall be the asylum for the unfortunate, that they may learn of manhood; the refuge of the oppressed, that they may learn of freedom; the grand theatre of noblest national virtues, and loftiest national character, wherein all mankind shall evermore rejoice. We must be faithful to our homes. Out of these homes shall go Christian mechanics, who shall do their work in life with a manly Christian love for God and for mankind, finding in it the greatest power for advancing the progress of the race; Christain teachers, filled and inspired with the wisdom that comes from above, and showing the way to a higher and nobler life; Christian reformers, all alive to the great responsibility of remoulding the character of social life and building up the social fabric in the spirit of a Christian love; Christian merchants, of unswerving and upright integrity, teaching all the nations of the world, as they meet in the course of trade, that commerce is the great force of civilization, and the unity of mankind the great truth of human life; Christian statesmen, of manly integrity, fearless for the right, working for all future time, and not merely for the present exigency — not sacrificing to party what was meant for mankind — spending and being spent in the work of raising a Christian commonwealth, to be the leader of the nations, the herald of the coming of the kingdom of God. There is nothing of good within the range of possibility which can not be accomplished by the influence of Christian homes!

Think of what we have now. The blessings of New-England — her thrift, her advanced civilization, her popular education, her freedom of thought, conscience, religion — came in a great measure from the homes of her early days. It was because the Pilgrims brought their homes with them, that they have made so deep an impress upon the character and history of the nation. It is because now of the homes that cluster beneath the shadow of her mountains, around the borders of her beautiful lakes, upon the slopes of her free hills, along the shores of her sounding sea; it is because now of the true men and women that are raised in those homes that she has produced a community that conquers her sterile soil and her unequal climate, and makes her name respected and honored through all the earth!

Let us see to it, my brothers, that we bequeath this honored home and the blessings of which it is the synonym to the future, stained by no wrong, sullied by no deed of wicked infidelity or dark iniquity, but brightened and enriched by our constancy and loyalty and truth.

III. THE YOUNG MAN IN SOCIETY.

The subject, which follows in natural course from that to which we last gave our attention, is The Social Duties of Young Men, or The Young Man in Society.

Society, in all civilized communities, has two senses. One is the narrow sense, which has reference to one's association with friends and acquaintances; the other, the wider sense, which belongs to the great combination of individual thoughts, emotions, purposes, plans, principles, words and deeds. That combination is not limited to one's familiar circle, but embraces all persons in the community. The thought and deed of each one contribute to or detract from the general good. When they have the character of evil, they become social evils, which affect more or less every man, woman and child, to their harm. When they have the character of good, they benefit every man, woman and child, and produce what we call the peace and good order of society. When they become criminal, they array against themselves the power of the state, and become amenable to the law. So we have all the paraphernalia of justice to protect society from all its dangerous classes. Against a petty theft, as against a terrible murder, the whole power of the state is evoked, and must inflict punishment, because the rights of property and the protection of life are matters in which not one man alone but all persons are interested.

The first thing which each one of us learns is, that we are dependent upon one another. This is the fact which is at the basis of society; namely, mutual dependence. It becomes, therefore, impossible to separate ourselves from social influences. There is not a single person, of whatever condition, character or class, that we may see at our homes, or meet in the street, with whom we are not in some way connected; from whom we do not receive or to whom we do not impart some good or ill. There is a kindred nature in us all, which we can not deny without injury to ourselves and to all others with whom we have intercourse. Our social distinctions, our regard for birth and caste, are in a great measure conventional and artificial. When we elevate them to a position and give them a character which do not really belong to them; when by them we attempt to cut off our connection with human life around us, we do violence to that humanity which is common to us all. When we use them, as we may, for accomplishing the benefit of those who are dependent upon us; when we acknowledge the family relationship which unites us with all God's children, and are faithful to it, we are giving a wider scope and a loftier stature to our manhood. We grow more generous and worthy by resolutely combatting every prejudice, which we find governing our action toward those of a different social position from our own, and by remembering, and always living as though we remembered it, that "of one blood, God created all nations of men to dwell on the face of the earth." We become selfish and unworthy of ourselves when we attempt to isolate our sympathies and contract the feelings of our soul; when from any unwillingness, or from any moral cowardice, we refuse to grant to others that meed of commendation, or that common interest which is their due. We must always acknowledge, we must always be faithful to, the bonds which join us. If God has made us brethren, we can not with impunity sever the connection.

Indeed, no man, however determined upon independence he may be, lives, or can live to himself. I have read of one who was so persistent in his determination of individual independence as to refuse the very simplest office of kindness from every one about him. Yet this man, suffering from some accident that befell him in the street, was carried to his home upon a shutter by an Irish hod-carrier, from whom, least of all, would he have received a helpful service. The most lonely and solitary position is by no means beyond the reach of providential and human companionship. Not one, even, of those old Christian devotees, in the early times of the church, who fled from the haunts of men, and sought the caves amid the distant crags of

Sinai, or dwelt in the vast solitudes of African deserts; of those monks of a later time, who shut themselves in cloistered convents to say their prayers and count their beads, and pass their lives in unbroken and devout meditation, thinking to do God service and grow to holiness of soul; of those of our own day, who leave their fellows and build their dwellings in the depth of the forest, but has found it impossible to free himself from his dependence upon others — a dependence, which, while it taught him his weakness, taught him also his manhood, and that he best serves himself who serves his fellow-men. Whittier, in his matchless verse, tells a story of a Theban monk, who, one day, at his meditations, near his desert cell, found a little child by his side, asking him what he did in the drear wilderness. At the hermit's answer, that here he worshipped God —

> "Alone with him, in this great calm
> I live, not by the outward sense —
> My will his love, my sheltering palm
> His providence,—
>
> "The child gazed round him. 'Does God live
> Here only? Where the desert's rim
> Is green with corn — at noon and eve,
> We worship him.'"

And then he tells the lonely man of his quiet home by the bank of the Nile, and so impresses him with the tale that he leads him away from his solitude to an humble cottage by the river-side and shows him his mother — strange to relate—the anchorite's own sister. Taught by thy child, says the monk—

> "Taught by thy child, whom God has sent,
> That love is more than fast or prayer,
> I come — toil, care and pain, content
> With thee to share.
>
> "Even as his foot the threshold crossed,
> The hermit's better life began ;
> Its holiest saint the Thebaid lost,
> And found a man."

True, indeed, solitude has its uses. We must sometimes be alone. Our own deepest experiences are only for ourselves to know. We need to go away from the noise and bustle of the world, to seek in quiet self-communings, and in lonely meditation that rest and peace which we do not find amid the public excitements of life. Every earnest life is impelled at times into solitude. Every true man feels himself at times alone. It is no fiction, that of the education of the desert, which the prophets had in Hebrew times—which strengthened the rugged spirit of John the Baptist — which taught Christ himself to resist and overcome temptation. We have to learn to stand by ourselves, and, by the spiritual energy of our own souls, work out our salvation and learn how to be really men. Yet this is so, or should be so, not from any morbid repugnance to the society of our fellow-men, but that we may more truly do our duty toward them, growing to the very best character by ourselves; making the most of what we have, and educating ourselves to the greatest possible extent, in order that by so doing, we may be better and more efficient workers upon society. We must never allow the opinions of others to control us; but we must form our opinions by ourselves and for ourselves, and give them voice and currency in the world, if they are of value enough to be received as the pure coin of origina thought. The celebrated Zimmerman, writing upon this subject, truly says: "The pleasures of society, though they may be attended with unhappy effect and pernicious consequences to men of weak heads and corrupted hearts, who only follow them for the purpose of indulging the follies and gratifying the vices to which they have given birth, are yet capable of affording to the wise and virtuous a high, rational, sublime and satisfactory enjoyment. The world is the only theater upon which great and noble actions can be performed, or the heights of moral and intellectual excellence usefully attained." He declares the design of his book upon solitude to be "to exhibit the necessity of combining the uses of solitude with those of society; to show in the strongest light the advantages they mutually derive from each other; to caution mankind of the danger of running into either extreme; to teach the advocate of uninterrupted society how highly all the social virtues may be improved and its vices easily abandoned by habits of solitary abstraction; and the advocate for continual solitude, how much that indocility and arrogance of character, which is contracted by a total absence from the world, may be corrected by the urbanity of society."

Beginning, therefore, at the young man's connection with society in its more limited sense, the first subject which is to be considered is, Manners. It is a word which can hardly be defined, yet it is always upon our lips, and from the difficulty of definition, it is only incumbent upon me to present a few suggestions. Manners and morals are said to be derived from the same original word. And as good morals are not merely outside acts of goodness, but must spring from good principles in the soul, so good manners are not the mere external adornments which a man or woman puts on simply to please, but must have their source in a true and loving heart. A gentleman is by no means made up of fashionable dress, and correct deportment, and faultless carriage in the drawing-room or at the table, though these are all matters which he would not wish to neglect. But there is something underneath the dress and the behavior — a manly and generous heart. In mere appearance, a fop can do as well as, or perhaps better than, a gentleman, and yet be nothing but a fop. Put him into any thing else but fine clothes, and you soon discover the difference. He can not behave properly, except when he is, so to speak, "got up" properly. Shakspeare gives a good description of a fop of his day, which, with one or two exceptions will answer well for a description of the same creature in our day. Hotspur describes him as they met after a battle —

> "A certain lord, neat, trimly dressed,
> Fresh as a bridegroom; and his chin new reaped,
> Showed like a stubble land at harvest-home.
> He was perfumed like a milliner;
> And 'twixt his finger and his thumb he held
> A pouncet-box, which, ever and anon,
> He gave his nose. . . . And still he smiled and talked.
> And as the soldiers bore dead bodies by,
> He called them, — untaught knaves, unmannerly,
> To bring a slovenly, unhandsome corse
> Betwixt the wind and his nobility.
> He made me mad
> To see him shine so brisk and smell so sweet,
> And talk so like a waiting gentlewoman;
> And that it was great pity, so it was,
> That villainous saltpetre should be digged
> Out of the bowels of the harmless earth,
> Which many a good tall fellow had destroyed,
> So cowardly; and, but for these vile guns,
> He would himself have been a soldier."

Put a gentleman into a homespun frock, and set him to work upon the farm or on the highway, and he is just as much a gentleman as ever, because his gentlemanliness belongs to his soul, not to his dress. His apparel is suited to the business he has in hand, and if we should go to see him, he will not apologize for his dress, nor bid us wait till he has changed it, for we do not wish to see and converse with the fine coat, but the brave heart and the gentle soul. Genuine politeness, too, can not be learned from books. It is not made of formalism and ceremonial proprieties, for these are outside, while real politeness is inward, not outward. Even fashion itself has to succumb sometimes to real manliness, and to confess that all its rules of behavior are good for nothing beside the simplicity and gentleness of truth. "A sainted soul," says Emerson, "is always elegant, and, it will pass unchallenged into the most guarded ring. But so will Jock the teamster pass, in some crisis, that brings him thither, and find favor, so long as his head is not giddy with the new circumstance, and the iron shoes do not wish to dance in waltzes and cotillons. The laws of behavior yield to the energy of the individual. The maiden at her first ball, the countryman at a city dinner, believes that there is a ritual, according to which every act and compliment must be performed, or the failing party must be cast out of this presence. Later, they learn, that good sense and character make their own forms every moment, and speak, or abstain, take wine or refuse it, stay or go, sit in a chair, or sprawl on the floor with the children, or stand on their head, or what else soever, in a new and aboriginal way; and that they will be always in fashion, let who will be unfashionable." Of course, it must always be understood that it is the character of the man that is able to support and make up for any deficiency in dress. Benjamin Franklin astonished the courtiers of Louis XVI. by appearing at court in the plain civilian's dress which he was accustomed to wear at home. He did not choose to bedizen himself with gold lace and embroidery, but dressed simply and naturally, as became himself and the land to which he belonged. But then it was Benjamin Franklin who did this. A man of less soul could not have done it. There are some men, and women too, indeed, who need fine clothes, and gold lace, and the display of barbaric jewels; and if they find that it makes up for internal deficiencies of character, we must be willing to grant them the harmless display without envy. Meantime, the true man can eat from wood or plain delf, and sit upon a hard bench, and dress in plain garments, and be no less true on that account. And, we are to remember, too,—for I would do justice to both sides—that while dress does not make a gentleman, so it does not unmake one. Because a man is finely and elegantly dressed, it does not follow that he is nothing more than a fop. A true and manly heart may beat beneath broadcloth and gay trimmings as beneath homespun and linsey-woolsey. At any rate, a man must not dress shabbily for the sake of showing that he is not a fop, but he must always dress as richly and elegantly as he can afford. The best dressed man or woman is he or she who occasions no remark but commendation for simplicity and neatness. We can not, therefore, lay down any law. Each man must act out his own feelings and convictions, taking care that these shall be truthful and just, and never allow his own distinctiveness and personality of character to be lost. "Some men's behavior," says Lord Bacon, "is like a verse wherein every syllable is measured; how can a man comprehend great matters that breaketh his mind too much to small observations? Not to use ceremonies at all is to teach others not to use them again, and so diminisheth respect to himself; but the dwelling upon them and exalting them above the moon is not only tedious, but doth diminish the faith and credit of him that speaks."

As good manners are not altogether subject to rule, nor to be learned except by practice, they become the result of intercourse with the world — with cultivated and noble men and women — with generous thought and pure purposes, as expressed in actual life. They become, also, the result of self-culture in the best moral and spiritual accomplishments.

1. First of all, it is evident, good manners can only be the outgrowth of good minds and souls. Even uncouthness and ignorance of the ways of the world may be glorified by a really good heart, as dull and unpleasant places often shine out in beauty beneath the influence of summer sunbeams. Incorrectness of speech even, does not obscure the radiant loveliness which gleams from a pure spirit, and we need have little fear that a gentle and loving heart will not show itself in gentle and loving ways. Such ways can never

be indications of ill-breeding. They rather are the substance of all true politeness. A morose, sullen, ill-tempered, passionate man is never a gentleman, and no contact with society, or intercourse with the world, or practice of pretty and complimentary phrases, can make him any thing but ill-bred. Self-control is among the first requisites of good manners. Just as surely as temper comes out in the quick, passionate, profane word, and the eye flashing with resentment upon any petty provocation, just so surely does ill-mannerliness come out with them. For anger and profanity are always vulgar. First of all, the movements of the heart and soul should be conducted gently and lovingly, if you wish to acquire good manners.

2. Truthfulness of soul is essential to good manners. A falsehood is always impolite, because falsehood is unmanly and immoral. If our intercourse rests on such a basis, and we call it politeness, we are dealing in shams and lies. We must learn always to tell the truth in a manly and open way. No young man should ever be a sneak or a coward. If he has any thing to say to a friend, let him do it, as one man should to another. If he chooses to write his thoughts, let him append his name in full, and never resort to those most cowardly of all things—anonymous letters. This does not diminish any obligation of courtesy or civility. The most searching and truthful words can always be spoken politely and courteously. This rule, indeed, we should provide, "that our truthfulness be full

of kindness and our kindness full of truth." Then every man should be true to himself, and never attempt to seem what he manifestly is not. We are too apt, I think, to give ourselves "airs," as we call them, which we can not support, and become affected where we should be natural and true. And this, I think, is not a peculiarity of one sex alone. Let every man and woman be simply true to his and her own thoughts, and express them naturally, and the ease and composure which belong to good manners will certainly be attained. Then every one should have self-respect. One reason why we make so many mistakes in life, is because we do not respect ourselves enough. We have not a genuine, hearty regard for the manhood within us. Self-respect always represses boldness and rudeness; will not permit us to do aught that is unmanly or mean, nor aught that is unworthy of our manhood. What we are is greater than what we do, and we should ever remember that, wherever we may be.

3. Another requisite of good manners is a deep reverence for God and a genuine regard for every man's humanity. True religion is true politeness, because it prevents vulgarity; it teaches that there is a reverent attitude of the soul which is always gentlemanly; it teaches us to revere that immortal character of human life which makes us akin to angels and to God. A true gentleman is kind and civil and courteous to every body, rich or poor, and never forgets that he is addressing one to whom belongs a power of spiritual

energy which all the influences of time and earth can not conquer. Washington, than whom no manlier man ever lived in America, while President, was walking one day through the streets of Philadelphia, with a friend, and met a poor black man, who, recognizing him, raised his hat, with a polite bow. The chief immediately returned the salutation. "Do you touch your hat to a negro?" asked his companion. "Certainly, sir," replied the General; "I should not wish to have him outdo me in politeness." There are some men who think politeness thrown away upon the poor and unfortunate. There can be no greater mistake. A kind and civil word is never thrown away, and the very poorest man knows when he is treated politely, and will be thankful for the kindness. There are some men, too, who think that politeness is not needed so much at home as abroad. They dress for strangers and are courteous to strangers, but when they are at home they change their politeness into harshness and severity, as they change their dress; thinking that the fact of kindred gives them a license to make all around them as uncomfortable as possible. "There is no place," says some English writer, "where real politeness is of more value than where we mostly think it would be superfluous."

There is a false politeness which is simply on the outside, and is an assumption, without any sincerity of character. Some hide behind their manners a false and black and deceitful heart. George IV., of England, was called, in his time, the "first gentleman of Europe," yet nevertheless was he the greatest debauchee in Europe. We all know how a man can "smile and murder while" he smiles. And Shakspeare declares that the Prince of Darkness himself was "a fine gentleman."

One has to learn, too, in this respect, that too much politeness of this kind is oftentimes as bad as too little. One can be overbred, and, by constant formality and ceremony, put all who come in contact with him as ill at ease and discomposed as though he had treated them in a rude and brusque way. Superfluous ceremony is far from polite. The true gentleman is he, the true lady is she, who takes the middle course; who puts every one at ease with whom he or she converses or deals; is affable, without familiarity; kind, without formality; dignified, without stiffness; cordial, frank and friendly always: — who always remembers, too, that each man and woman, whatever their position or condition, are to be treated in a gentle and Christian way, and this because they all belong to the same great family.

Montaigne, a famous French essayist, says very truly: "I have seen some men rude by being over civil, and troublesome by their courtesy, though, these excesses excepted, the knowledge of courtesy and good manners is a very necessary study. It is, like grace and beauty, that which begets liking and inclination to love one another at the first sight, and in the very beginning of an acquaintance and familiarity; and consequently, that which first opens the door for us to better ourselves by the example of others, if there be any thing in society worth our notice."

But to leave this part of my subject, let us consider the young man's relations to society in a wider sense. There are duties to perform, as well as pleasures to enjoy, in social life. God made no one of us for a selfish indolence. He did not bestow upon us these noble powers without giving us also noble opportunities for using them. If we have strength, it is that we should help the weak; knowledge, that we should use it for the benefit of our fellow-creatures; wealth, that we should be faithful to it, as stewards of his bounty; position and power, that we should occupy them for the welfare of all who are dependent upon us for happiness. Thus, mutually dependent, we must be mutually helpful. Being members one of another, we should bear one another's burdens. This is no less a duty of social life than of the Christian religion. Our limited sense of society is joined to our wider sense. For we have to learn not only to be true gentlemen in the parlor and the drawing-room, but also to be true Christian men in the street, and among those ranks of social life which are to be uplifted and blessed by our fidelity. In the times of chivalry, he who would wear the honors of knighthood was obliged, as the champion of God and woman, to devote himself "to speak the truth, to maintain the right, to protect the distressed, to practice courtesy, to despise the allurements of ease and safety, and to vindicate in every perilous adventure the honor of his character." And the knight of old was no less brave in the field, because he was gallant and courteous in lady's bower. He who would be chivalric and knightly now, may well take a lesson from those old times, and practice the same virtues which made them heroic.

Looking out, then, upon social life as it exists beyond the immediate circle of one's own acquaintance, what do we see? Society is by no means pervaded by a Christian sentiment, or entirely governed by it, though it is so in a great measure. Mankind, though in the way of progress, have not attained in any direction to a complete control over their circumstances. Here, in our own country, with millions upon millions of acres of the most fruitful land waiting for the husbandman, there is poverty to freezing and starving. Here, where there is but comparatively little to stimulate the appetite, and where innocent pleasures are within the reach of all, there are self-indulgence and intemperance unparalleled in any country on the face of the globe. Here, with our free institutions, with the best system of government ever devised by man, and the grandest opportunity for applying it to national life, with our democratic theory of the equality of mankind, there is slavery, staining the fair fame of the republic, corrupting the national character, and defiling and debasing us all.

To every young man entering life these questions inevitably present themselves — how to relieve and prevent poverty, how to put an effectual check to the terrible evils of intemperance, how to hasten the day when the fetters shall be stricken from the limbs of the slave, and the genuine democratic American idea of justice for all, liberty for all, shall be realized. I say, inevitably present themselves, because, being mutually dependent upon each other, the good or evil of one class and condition of men affects all classes and conditions. No one escapes. As soon as we enter into active life, we are compelled, from the very nature of the case, to give our influence and work to one side or the other of these questions, and to be either for or against. Evil does not simply affect those alone who are its immediate victims — it touches us all with its deadly hand. There is no such thing as localizing evil. Its influence is in the air, and poisons it; it is in the earth, and makes it sterile; it is a shadow in every sunbeam; it is a blasting influence upon every labor. Industry is weakened. Thought, conscience, religion, are paralyzed by it. How quickly does it taint and envenom the fresh life of youth, quenching its generous emotion, and with iron hand crushing its love for truth, and liberty, and God!

On the other hand, how quick and vitalizing is the influence of good. Fill the social state with benevolence, with self-control, with noble thoughts and aims, with humanity and truthfulness; let the air be all electric with ideas of right, with an unconquerable regard for justice, with an unwavering love of freedom, and what blessings and happiness belong to it. Public opinion on the right side is omnipotent. "It is able," said Mr. Webster once, "to oppose the most formidable obstruction to the progress of injustice and oppression; and as it grows more intelligent and more intense, it will be more and more formidable. It may be silenced by military power, but it can not be conquered. It is elastic, irrepressible, and invulnerable to the weapons of ordinary warfare. It is that impassible, unextinguishable enemy to mere violence and arbitrary rule, which, like Milton's angels, 'vital in every part, can not but by annihilation die.'" Nothing is more true, or could be more forcefully put than this. Yet are we not too ready to separate ourselves from this public opinion, and speak of it as some power outside of us? We forget that public opinion is nothing more than the combination of individual opinions. My opinion, and your opinion, what we think and say individually, all go to make up public opinions, and so we ourselves are personally responsible to a great degree for the character of public opinion. Only let us think truly and correctly, and say what we think boldly!

1. As the young man goes out, then, to grapple with the evils of life, to determine his position and decide where he will stand, and whether manfully or cowardly he will do his work there, the first and most obvious duty is, that he should go out with well-

established principles and strong convictions of duty. Fully convinced of his responsibility, and always remembering that the welfare of others, as well as his own, is depending upon his fidelity, let him go with fearlessness, fully resolved that, so far as he is concerned, society shall in no wise suffer from his neglect and wrong. In regard to these questions of social wrong, every young man is disposed at first to be a reformer. He looks out upon social life with the generosity that is natural to his time of life, and devotes himself at once to the work of relief and reform. There are, indeed, exceptions to this, for instances may be found where the fresh impulses of youth are bound in the stiffness of a formal conservatism, and the young man looks with scorn upon all attempts to realize a better state of things. But these are the results either of a false education, or a surrender of the soul to wrong principles, or a subjection to that heartless system which subordinates what is right to what is respectable. But, as a general thing, we can rely upon the young men. If uncorrupted by vice, and unaffected by false ideas of life, and unbought by venal ambition, we can rely upon the young men for an advocacy and support of those causes which have for their object an improvement in the condition of our social life. There is hardly one of you now here who does not feel that slavery, intemperance and vice are grievous wrongs, and that you have something to do with their correction. You would not be a drunkard, an oppressor, a tyrant. Thackeray well says: "A young man begins the world with some aspirations at least; he will try to be good, and follow the truth; he will strive to win honors for himself, and never do a base action; he will pass nights over his books, and forego ease and pleasure, that he may achieve a name. Many a poor wretch, who is worn out now, and old, and bankrupt of fame and money too, has commenced life at any rate with noble views and generous schemes, from which weakness, idleness, passion, or overpowering hostile fortune has turned him away." Thus it certainly is with most of us. But worldliness, vice, evil associations, and the influence of selfish maxims, check the impulse and erase the impression. Mature life comes on, and the man sinks down into his comforts and ease, content to let the evil go on and make its conquests, over himself as well as his fellow-men. The heartless and selfish principles of life have carried the day. What we must do, my brothers, is to carry first generous feelings with us through our whole lives; never to allow ourselves to grow old in our hearts; to resist the chilling influences of worldliness; to deepen our impulses to principles, and strengthen our early impressions, stamping them into our souls till they become convictions. True, we may see dishonesty and insincerity in the advocacy of the best enterprise, and find men playing the demagogue in the holiest of causes. Nevertheless is it our duty to see to it that we remain true to our principles; nevertheless must we approach these questions, and discuss them earnestly and fearlessly. We must not be cowards here, or we must not be elsewhere. We must be brave and true, "without fear and without reproach." Moral cowardice is the unmanliest of all things, and no attainment of learning, eloquence, position, can supply the deficiency which it causes in the soul. We must calmly and steadily stand against all wrong, faithfully performing the duty which we know we ought. Nevertheless, remembering what large results wait upon our faithful action, must we carry our fresh and vigorous life into the stagnant and corrupted ways of social life, and infuse a new vitality into the sluggish current, in which the old opinions too often run. We will not suffer ourselves to be deceived by the falsehoods of the hour. We will understand what is true and manly in human life, and make it greater by the addition to it of our own truth and manliness! This is our duty. Duty? It is our privilege! Let us use it well!

2. The young man must exercise care in the choice of his companions and friends. As he desires to save himself from evil and grow in virtue, he finds that he is drawn to others, or that he draws them to himself, to help him in the work. And so the question, who his associates shall be, is a very important one. The influence of companions, though not always perceptible, is yet most powerful. "As iron sharpeneth iron," says a Hebrew proverb, "so a man sharpeneth the countenance of his friend." It is said that different persons

who live together gradually come into resemblance to each other, not only in mind and character, but also in physical features. We all know how easily thoughts, feelings, language, tones of voice, become contagious. This is an influence which all exert and receive, and none resist. And thus we are all affected, more or less, by the company we keep. The difference between well and ill bred men — though some allowance is to be given to that natural refinement which shines out from the rags of poverty, or that natural vulgarity which no amount of wealth can conceal, yet — is created to a great degree by the difference of associations. And in other respects the same result is perceptible. The society of the good purifies, the society of the evil corrupts, the moral nature. A really good man sends out from himself virtue; surrounds himself with a warm, and genial, and kindly atmosphere. When you come within the reach of his influence, you can not help receiving a benefit; when you go away from it, you can not but carry a blessing. An evil man sends out a vicious influence; surrounds himself with an atmosphere of evil, to which it is dangerous to be exposed. As we need preventives and antidotes when we go into an atmosphere infectious with disease, so we need moral preventives and antidotes against the contagion of evil association. It is said that some soldiers have worn a shirt of mail beneath their ordinary uniforms, of so fine a texture and of so exquisite a temper, as to be impervious to bullet and impenetrable by sword, while it in no wise impeded the slightest movement of limb or body. I think we need something like this in our moral conflicts — an armor of righteous principle, which shall never obstruct our action in any good enterprise, while it shall insure our safety in the warmest part of the battle.

What may give importance to what I have just said, is the fact that the most dangerous temptations which a young man has to deal with are those which allure, not drive him to destruction. They come in the guise of what is called good fellowship. The open and generous temperament, which, if rightly directed, would make a noble man, is moved by them and is ruined by them. They appeal to one's sympathy, and sensibilities, and love of companionship. He listens to their seductive tones. The harmonies of their song fall pleasantly upon the ear. He sinks before he is aware into the soft embraces of pleasure, which kill out the energy of his soul. In the old mythology, three Siren sisters inhabited an island near the south-western coast of Italy, where, by their singing, they caught the attention of the passing mariners. No voices in the world but one so potent and so sweet as theirs; no songs but those of Orpheus so ravishing in their delightful measures. No one who heard them could resist their fascinating strains. But they sang to allure the hapless sailor to a swift destruction. Even the brave Ulysses, returning from the siege of Troy, though he met unarmed all other dangers, and conquered them, did not dare to pass the enchanting spot without some precautions. He stopped the ears of his rowers with wax, that they could not hear, and then commanded them to bind him with strongest chains to the mast of his galley, that he, though hearing, might not be able to break away from the restraint.

> "Then the sweet charmers warbled o'er the main;
> My soul takes wing to meet the heavenly strain,
> I give the sign, and struggle to be free,
> Swift row my mates and shoot along the sea;
> New chains they add, and rapid urge the way,
> Till, dying off, the distant sounds decay;
> Then, scudding swiftly from the dangerous ground,
> The deafened ear unlocked — the chains unbound."

This was effectual, but it was not the bravest way. That way was found by Orpheus, who, when the Argonauts, in whose company he was, sailed over that sea, drowned the Sirens' music by a sweeter song, and saved his companions by filling their ears with purer melody. And so the young man of the present day, as he hears the strains of pleasure and of vice, and their alluring voices, should be ready with a better and more enchanting music — the music of a soul which is filled with the pure affection of a Divine love, and the power of a manly purpose. He, too, sails over the sea. Guided by a true principle, and laying his course by the chart of duty, he shall be able to shun the many dangers that will meet him, and seize at last the Golden Fleece of virtue!

I think the most dangerous associate for a young man is what is called a companionable man, of loose principles, or no principles at all. He is a man of wit, fascinating in conversation, full of soft flatterings, calls himself a gentleman, is proficient in all the mysteries of the gaming table, borrows your money, if you are foolish enough to lend it, or cheats you out of it, if you are silly enough to play. He knows all your weak points, is ready with just the right word at the right moment to entice you to indulgence, and garnishes his wickedness with the proprieties and even the graces of life. He is all things to all men, that he may ruin some. He will talk religion with saintly decorousness to a clergyman, politics to a lawyer, literature to a scholar, scandal to a gossip, agreeable nonsense and empty compliment to a coquette, general news to a man of the world, and unspeakable vileness to the vile. The whole vocabulary of pleasure is at his command. But he is a knave, a drunkard, a libertine, a scoundrel. Never let us allow ourselves to be deceived by the external adornments which this man puts on. Judge his character for what it is worth, and shun his company as you would the most poisonous of reptiles. Many a young man, aye, many a young woman, has fallen a victim to the enticements of such a man. Many a course of infamy dates back for its beginning to such companionship. Do not trust in his proposals, for he has nothing to offer but the momentary gratification of convivial enjoyment and the unhealthy carousal. Nothing more? Ah yes—sadly a great deal more. The listless stupidity that follows the revel—the terrible void of a want unsatisfied—the bitter reproaches of an injured and violated conscience—the awful voice of self-condemnation echoing through the empty chambers of the soul—and the consciousness of ruin and despair! And all this must be borne in secret and alone; for it is not the man who has accomplished the work of destruction, who relieves when calamity comes, who whispers consolation in distress, who attempts to comfort the weary heart, who would smooth the way to the grave. He has nothing to give then. He has done his work, and seeks new victims. There is every thing to lose, and nothing to gain, in such association!

But, it may be said, one must go into the company of others for the sake of benefiting them. I agree to that. It is a real missionary work to go among the fallen and raise them up; to go among the abandoned, and reclaim them. It is true philanthropy to lift up the helpless and weak, and give them power worthily to do their work in the world. Let it be the motive, and let young men go to this work with a strong and right principle, and with such a pure purpose that no contact with impurity shall defile them, and undoubtedly the best results would follow. Social duties would be faithfully performed, and the world made better.

Avoiding evil associations, let the young man seek

the company of the wise, the virtuous, and the good. There is something noble in an association of young men for mutual improvement; that, by so educating themselves, they may do their work faithfully to those around them; that they may grow in mental and moral power; that they may repel those influences of evil which repress their enthusiasm and deaden their sympathies; that, by helping each other, they may learn to help those of different association and condition. Improvement—that is the word—improvement of one's self, that others may be improved; that your love of all things true and just may be quickened; that your compassion for the poor, the unfortunate, the destitute, the slave, may be made stronger; that you may never become heartless, selfish, worldly, and false; that your souls may be enlarged to all right endeavor and all worthy enterprise; and that you may be chivalric and brave in the service of humanity, for helping the distressed, for encouraging the feeble, for being manly, Christly and godly, in this present world.

And here we find that the man who is faithful to society, as we view it in its widest and highest sense, is faithful to society in its lower sense. He is the true gentleman. If he has polish and refinement and cultivation, it is that he may the better serve the welfare of his fellow-men. He shows that a man may bear himself no less gracefully in the saloons of fashion, because he keeps himself true to virtue—because he has an ear quick to hear the cry of sorrow—because he has a hand ready to relieve the wanting and the weak. The polish of his nature is not the hard enamel which spreads its flinty gloss over every fine emotion, but that process which brings out the hidden beauties and virtues of the soul. I protest against that nomenclature which attempts to dignify any vice by calling it gentlemanly, and that would give it a currency and importance by introducing it into polite society. It is no less a vice because it is fashionable; and, however fashionable it may be, it never can become gentlemanly. Vice is always vice; though you may dress it in fine clothes, and put pretty words upon its lips, and teach it graceful attitudes, it is no less vice. You can not redeem it thus from its innate and vicious vulgarity. To become intoxicated at an evening party, or in a college society room, is no more respectable than in a drinking cellar. Gambling at Baden-Baden, though the table be surrounded by *blasé* European noblemen, and unsophisticated young Americans, seeing the world, is no more noble nor less disgraceful than at a New-York "hell." Licentiousness and domestic infidelity are always vulgar and never gentlemanly, though they may happen to be importations direct from Paris. Slavery is never chivalric, never generous, and never civilized. It is always mean, and cowardly, and brutal, and barbarous, whatever airs of assumption, and breeding, and exclusiveness, plantation manners at Washington and elsewhere may put on. Let us call things by their right names, and then we shall know that the true gentleman is a man of stainless honor, of unsullied virtue, of knightly generosity, of delicate sensibility, of pure purpose, and of Christly compassion. St. Paul was a gentleman when he said, "Be not drunk with wine, wherein is excess;" and, "Bear ye one another's burdens." And the old writers with no less reverence than truth called Christ the truest gentleman that ever lived. And he said, "Inasmuch as ye give bread to the hungry, and clothes to the naked, ye do it unto me." Let us not be deceived. A true Christian man, who keeps himself from all things vile, and gives himself to the service of all things just, is the true gentleman!

Let each one of us be that brave and true Christian man. Let us have firm convictions of duty and of right, and fixed principles of action. Then what we know to be just and true, let us speak it, let us do it, come whatever may. Do we not need some of that spirit of self-devotion which was in the martyrs and the Apostles? that we, as they, may face all obloquy and persecution, and death, if that be necessary, without the quiver of an eyelid, without the blanching of a cheek, or the trembling of a lip — true in all things and through all things to our honest thought? Do we not need more of that moral courage which dares be right when wrong is popular — which dares be true when falsehood prevails in high places and low —

which dares pursue the straightforward course of rectitude through conflicts and agitations, when the world cries out in approval of a crooked policy, and bravely hold one's own position when men demand a selfish surrender to wrong for the sake of quiet and peace? Be not pretentious and forward, but calmly and resolutely faithful to righteous convictions, allowing no power to move you from them; and thus persistently fight the battle which must be fought, and patiently wait till the popular power comes, and the world comes round to you, to aid in the hour of victory! This we do need—this we can have. Keep, then, young man, your sympathies warm, fresh, and living. Remember that others' good is depending upon your fidelity to principle, and true in all things and through all things, be the member of society which you know you can be, and which you know you should be!

Need I say more? Let not my words speak, but listen to the voices which come up from the world's dark places of misery and woe. Hear the lamentations of the poor—hear the cries that come for help from sad and broken hearts—hear what comes from the drunkard's wretched home—from the cabin of the slave, from the abodes of wretchedness and want, asking for sympathy and relief. Ask your own warm heart, and listen to the answer which it gives. Is it one of indolence, of heartlessness, and selfishness? Oh no, not that, but an answer of work, manly, steady, vigorous work, for the benefit of God's children—your brothers and mine!

"A sense of an earnest will
 To help the lowly-living —
 And a terrible heart-thrill
 If you have no power of giving:
 An arm of aid to the weak,
 A friendly hand to the friendless,
 Kind words, so short to speak,
 But whose echo is endless :—
The world is wide — these things are small,
They may be nothing, but they are all!"

"Let us go forth, and resolutely dare
With sweat of brow to toil our little day —
Our hearts to God! To brother-man,
Aid, blessing, labor, prayer!"

IV. THE YOUNG MAN IN BUSINESS.

The subject which I have proposed for this evening's consideration, is The Young Man in Business.

I use the word Business here to denote all the various branches of labor to which the young man is called, as he goes out into life. God has so ordered our life as to make it evident that he intended us to arrive at the development of our various faculties by means of labor. Indolence and idleness are found by actual experience to be full of mischievous results. With vacant mind and soul, superadded to vacant hands, the life of a man becomes worthless and inefficient. He is a consumer and no producer, and inasmuch as he refuses thus to do his part toward adding to the possessions or fruits of human industry — he becomes a cumberer of the ground. I can conceive of nothing more miserable than a fruitless and unproductive life, with nothing in the retrospect to give satisfaction, and nothing in the prospect to inspire hope. It is also contrary to the course of human progress. All advancement in all ages has been accomplished only by unceasing labor. We now rejoice in myriads of blissful results.

It is because through all the past men have faithfully worked — worked in unselfish and generous spirit — worked with persevering constancy — worked with high and true aims. We now have entered into their labors and enjoy the fruits of their faithfulness. Had they folded their hands in listless idleness, or despairingly fled from the field of human labor, we should have been poor, and miserable, and naked. We owe it to the future, as, indeed, it is the only way in which we can pay our debt of gratitude to the past — we owe it to the future to work as bravely and manfully in our generation as the fathers did in theirs, with the same high ideals and the same abundant successes.

Indeed, labor is a necessity. We are compelled to work. No good thing has ever been obtained without it, and no good can be obtained without it. If to be wise we must study, to be strong we must labor. If God has given us minds and bodies, if he has given us heads and hands, he undoubtedly intended that we should accomplish some result by means of them. They were not given in vain, or without a purpose. We have the whole earth before us to conquer. Nature has forces, which we are to bring into use for supplying our necessities. The sky and the air are full of powers, which, by proper diligence and labor, we may secure for our wants; and there is no one of us but may add something to the sum of the world's good, by fidelity to the world's great laws of productive industry. Shall we ever be idle consumers? Look around us. God works and has worked through all ages for us. Nature works, never ceasing her ever wonderful though familiar processes. And if our fellow-men discontinued any of their labors we should be poor indeed. We can not eat a single meal of the the very simplest food, without calling into requisition the labors of many men in various parts of the earth. The clothes we wear were fashioned by a thousand hands. The books we read were produced by the intensest labor. There is no single object which we see that does not teach us a lesson of industrious toil, that does not rebuke our indolence, and that ought not to shame us out of our idle indulgence. In all this vast universe there is no man, however privileged he may be, that has a right to be a drone or a dependent!

To one's natural idleness is added a prejudice against labor, which is censurable. Young men sometimes think that it is not respectable to be at work. They imagine that there is some character of disgrace or degradation belonging to toil. No greater mistake could possibly be made. Instead of being disgraceful to engage in work, it is especially honorable. It is the useless man, not the useful man, who is in a condition of disgrace. It is the man who will do nothing; who eats the bread he does not earn; who relies upon others to support his life; it is he who is not respectable, because he is doing nothing to command respect. It is surprising to see how many young men there are at the present day who are growing up to habits of constant idleness. They are not always among the poor. They are to be found among the rich and fortunate classes. They are young men without business; giving no indications of preparation for a good or useful life; but rather preparing themselves for a manhood of sorrow, and an old age — if their habits of life will permit them to reach it — an old age of unavailing regrets, with its burden of remembered follies added to the infirmities of years. Their days and nights are spent in places of ill repute. Their object seems to be to kill time, not to use it. To them come the temptations which always belong to idleness. They must spend the weary hours in some way. They have no healthful stimulant of labor, no good occupation, to fill the day with satisfaction. They seek the excitements of the gaming table. They find a stimulant in intoxicating drink. Their moral life is corrupted. They are bankrupt in character. They are insolvent in soul. So lived not their fathers before them. They gained their position of competence by dint of untiring industry. They rose from humble places by unwearied industry. They now have the satisfaction of looking back upon an honorable course of life, and of enjoying the results which they have attained. But, unfortunately, they do not teach their children to follow in their footsteps. They allow them to look upon labor with aversion, at least, if not with absolute repugnance, and so train them, perhaps unwittingly, to courses which end only in shame. There is many a man, doubtless, now in middle life, who sorrowfully looks back upon his early days, which he has permitted to slip away without any good endeavors; who regrets the insufficiency of his early training; who laments that he has nothing to do; that he has learned no useful trade; that he has followed no honorable profession, and that his life is now wasted beyond retrieval. Now is the time, young man, to provide against such a sorrowful period. Do not allow yourself to grow up without any thing to do. Believe that a condition of idleness is the worst for you, and that any labor, that will furnish occupation for your mind and your hands, is better than a life which accomplishes nothing, and which will, by and by, be full of misery. Shun the gaming table. Break every bottle of wine you can find, and pour its contents into the sewer, which is a better place for it than your own stomach. Do not make yourself a slave to your horse, and go to work! I think you will find such a course better for you than the fortune which you expect to inherit by and by!

There is a little incident in the life of Plutarch, the famous biographer of the heroes of classic times, which in this connection is worth relating. It will show, I think, in what manner the loftiest souls regard the labors of life, and find no useful occupation without honor and dignity. It may seem menial to some, but useful and honest toil is never menial, and the smallest duty may be performed in such a spirit of genuine manhood as to make it noble. Plutarch, having acquired an enviable and indeed an immortal fame, as a philosopher and a man of consummate wisdom, left the polished and cultivated circles of Rome, in which he shone as a most brilliant member, where he had received the most distinguished honors, and even educated an emperor in wisdom and virtue, and returned to his native city of Chæronea, among the rude Bœotians. Here his townsmen elected him to fill many offices, among which was that of commissioner of sewers and public buildings. Upon such offices he is said to have looked "in the same light as the great Epaminondas had done, who, when he was appointed to a commission beneath his rank, observed, 'that no office could give dignity to him that held it, but that he who held it might give dignity to it.'" In regard to the particular office which I have just mentioned, Plutarch himself says: "I make no doubt that the citizens of Chæronea often smile when they see me employed in such offices as these. On such occasions I generally call to mind what is said of Antisthenes. When he was bringing home a dirty fish from the market, some who observed it expressed their surprise. 'It is for myself,' said he, 'that I carry this fish.' On the contrary, for my own part, when I am rallied for measuring tiles, and calculating a quantity of stones or mortar, I answer, that it is not for myself I do these things, but for my country. For in all things of this nature, the public utility takes off the disgrace; and the meaner the office you sustain, the greater is the compliment you pay to the public."

"The public utility takes off the disgrace," says the old philosopher. It is worth remembering. Whatever is useful to the public is honorable, and no man ought to be ashamed of his toil, if it is for the public benefit. One occupation is no more honorable than another, unless it produces larger and more beneficial results. The force and honor of character do not depend by any means upon occupation. John Pounds, a poor shoemaker in an English city, gathered poor children about him as he sat at work, and taught them to read, and that shoemaker's bench became prouder than an imperial throne. It is true manhood that always gives honor. Because I work with my head, and my neighbor with his hands, it by no means follows that I am more honorably employed than he. If I am of more public benefit than he, I am to be honored more. If he is of more public benefit than I, he is to be honored more. It is not a question as to who has the most money, who has the widest reputation, or who holds the highest office, but who accomplishes the most public good. And so the criterion of honor is usefulness. I think we all have to learn that we each have a place in God's universe, and that each in his place is able to work with benefit to God's universe. I think we have to learn, too, that where a man, in his place, is doing his work as A MAN, he is to be respected therefor, because he is doing it for the good of all mankind. When he refuses to do his work, as a man, he deserves to lose respect. Let no working man ever allow himself to despise his work, or allow others to despise it. God placed him where he is, and gave him the faculties which he has. His duty is, with self-respect and faithfulness, to do his work there as a child of God. An old Persian poet once well sang:

> "I saw some handfuls of the rose in bloom,
> With bands of grass suspended from a dome,
> I said — 'What means this worthless grass, that it
> Should in the rose's fairy circle sit?'
> Then wept the grass and said, 'Be still, and know
> The kind their old associates ne'er forego;
> Mine is no beauty, hue, or fragrance, true,
> But in the garden of my Lord I grew.'"

Another reason why honest labor is to be honored, is, that it is connected with all human progress. As I endeavored to show in my last lecture, we are all dependent upon one another in the social state; so, in this matter of labor, it is equally true that we never can be independent of each other. We help each other in our labors. It is because I do one kind of work, and my neighbor another, and this man still a different one, and that man another still, that so much is done on the whole. All the different interests of life are cared for, some by one body of men, and some by another, but all by some. Many men have many minds, and the many minds combined produce the great result desired. You have seen how, in a child's puzzle, there are numerous pieces, each unshapely and irregular in itself, but each fitting into the other; and all, brought together, as they should be, forming a complete and perfect geometrical figure, as a square, or circle, or triangle, or what not. In this mighty frame of things—to illustrate great things by small—where Providential plans of vastest extent come to their fulfillment by human agency, Providence, with infinite forecast, has given to each man a peculiar genius and skill, which, if exerted aright, will accomplish the best results. And all the different labors of men, though they may be dissimilar and various, fit into each other, and, in their proper combination, make up a complete and beautiful whole, and God's plans come to their fruition through the faithfulness and variety of human labor!

I. If these things are so, it becomes a duty, which the young man owes no less to society than to God and his own good, that he should adopt a business of some kind—that he should do something which will be of use and benefit to his fellow-men. To sustain himself—to be true to his God—to be faithful to the human life about him, he must have a fixed and settled vocation, and he must be industrious. This is the first thing. The Jews had one or two excellent maxims respecting this. One was: "What is commanded of a father toward a son? To circumcise him, to teach him the law; to teach him a trade." Another was: "He that hath a trade in his hand, is like a vineyard that is fenced."

And St. Paul said something of this kind: "If any would not work, neither should he eat; for we hear that there are some who walk among you disorderly, working not at all, but are busy-bodies. Now, them that are such, we command and exhort, by our Lord Jesus Christ, that with quietness they work and eat their own bread."

I was glad to find, not many months since, in one of the journals of the city of Providence, the following sensible remarks. They deserve to be written in letters of gold, and carried in the mind as a vade mecum by every young man, as he enters into active life:

"The benefit of a good mechanical trade, even to those whose fortunate position places them above the necessity of daily labor, can hardly be over estimated. The use of tools, the practice of planning and designing, the ability to work, are all sure to come into use, in a great variety of ways, and are pretty certain never to do a man any harm. An educated mechanic, a young man who has faithfully gone through the course of instruction in our public schools, and has learned a good trade, has in his head and in his hands a capital that no reverse of fortune can take away from him. There is no young man so favored by fortune, entering upon life with such high expectations, that the knowledge of a mechanical trade, at least so far as the use of tools and the ability to plan, should be a matter of indifference to him. The rich and the poor in our country are constantly interchanging, and passing from one class to the other. There is no security for retaining wealth, except the same habits and qualities that are necessary to its acquisition."

II. The young man, having thus observed the necessity of labor, the question comes to him in relation to the choice of his occupation. What particular trade shall he learn? What profession shall he study? What branch of business shall he undertake? It is evident, I think, that each one has some peculiar genius for some peculiar work. One has mechanical skill, another mental ability, another commercial genius. Plato, in his Republic, declares that "No two persons are born exactly alike, but each differs from the other in natural endowments, one being suited for one occupation and another for another; and all things will be produced in superior quantity and quality, and with greater ease, when each man works at a single occupation, in accordance with his natural gifts." This is true, and I think it is also true, that he will be successful in his occupation who pursues it faithfully, and being so successful, he thus best serves the State. The country loses a great many excellent farmers, and mechanics, and tradesmen, and suffers from an excess of poor professional men, and politicians, because the man in the first place has not ascertained for what he is best fitted. He thinks there is honor in the position, rather than in his own manhood, and so he seeks to fill the position rather than to be a man in all positions. He makes a great mistake; for the world generally judges a man by what he is, rather than by what he does. If he is manly and true he will receive respect, be his occupation what it may. If he is not manly or true, he will be despised as he deserves, whatever his position. Every man has justice done him sooner or later, and if he does a true and manly service, which benefits the world, he may be assured the world will not forget him. Let him do what he knows best, and do it in the best way he knows, and he need have little fear of a want of appreciation by his fellow-men. I have seen an account of a slight but very significant incident, which is said to have taken place during one of the annual sessions of the Methodist Conference of Maine. "On one of the evenings during the week of assembly, there was a good old-fashioned sermon preached by an old minister from the 'upper Kennebec country.' The preacher, in the dialect of his sect, evidently felt the 'reformation spirit,' and had a 'free utterance.' At the close of his stirring address he made an earnest appeal to those who were anxious to receive the mercy proffered, to come forward and take the front seats. While the members of the congregation were obeying his summons, he desired the brethren to sing a hymn. Accordingly one was started. Unfortunately, it was not familiar, and it dragged heavily. Few voices joined to swell its notes, and those were timid and weak. One wretched stanza was at last finished. Another was commenced with diminished vigor, if possible, the preacher all the while urging the anxious ones forward.

At last, however, he stopped, for the singing was growing fainter and fainter, so ill adapted was it to the occasion and his own feelings, gazed around upon the congregation for a moment, and then exclaimed from a full heart, 'Sing what you know, brethren! sing what you know!' A woman, with the quick perception of her sex, immediately struck up a more familiar tune, full of spirit and devotion. Hearts were touched all over the crowded house; scores joined in, the church was filled with melody and praise; and at the close a venerable minister, with a head as white as Mt. Washington in mid-winter, a kindly face, and a great warm heart, bowed before the altar, and offered up a prayer such as one only hears at a Methodist meeting." I apprehend it is a common cause of failure with us, that we try to sing what we do not know. The old minister gives us all excellent counsel; simply to sing what we know. Let us heed it well, and be successful in our heeding!

Another element here comes in to direct us in the choice of an occupation, besides peculiar genius which we have for a peculiar branch of industry. There must be something more than inclination entering into our purposes. There is the end, which we desire to secure. That end, of course, is success, and we are led at once into the inquiry as to the results involved in what we call a successful life. These results are almost as various as the different classes of occupations. A successful business man is generally a man who accumulates a fortune, and becomes rich; and, as we call it, independent. A successful politician is he who, by means of political management, obtains political preferment, and holds high office. A successful professional man is he who achieves a wide extended reputation and fame. But when we come fully to understand what is really meant by genuine manhood, and how much belongs to the fact of being a man; when we consider the wide extent and the vast power of the soul's faculties, we are led to think that success means somewhat more than the collection of wealth, the acquirement of office, or the achieval of reputation. When we have gained these, we have not gained every thing, and there must be something more than these to be regarded as the end of a true man's life. These are but means to a greater end. They find their value in their right use, and they become mischievous, and wrong, and wicked, when they are solely ends, and the powers of our manhood are devoted to their acquisition and to nothing more.

For, 1st, to become rich is not the best thing which a man can do. Sometimes the pursuit of wealth is accompanied by meanness, by fraud, by dishonesty, and then the man becomes miserly and loses his manhood. Sometimes it is accompanied by generosity, uprightness, and a true manly energy, and then wealth is honorable, for its accumulation has not overpowered the best faculties of the soul, but rather has developed them. For it requires industry, it requires perseverance, it requires vigilance, it requires a bold use of favorable opportunity, to acquire a competence. A lazy man, a vacillating and weak man, a sleepy man, a timid man can not become rich. He has not the power of moulding and controlling circumstances, and of seizing upon events, and using them with a strong and firm purpose. And so far as it does require the qualities which I have mentioned, the acquisition of property becomes an education of character; for the relations of business are wide and cosmopolitan, and train a man to thought and action. The remark of a wealthy citizen when asked how he made his money, is an illustration of the force of character which many rich men possess. "Sir, I understood my business and attended to it, and if I were to become poor again to-morrow, I could commence as an ash-man and make another fortune, if God spared my life and health to work." Yet, when virtue and integrity are sacrificed to the selfish acquisition of money, and the highest interests of human life are put in jeopardy in the labor, we very soon come to understand that there are other and better faculties of our nature, which such acquisition does not develop, and which it even endangers. And the fact that any particular business has in its result an ample fortune, is not the sole reason why a young man should choose to follow it. One of the most, or perhaps the most profitable business in our day is the manufacture of quack medicines. Yet, it does not follow that we should all engage in it, though we can do so, and be no less true and honest in that than in others. We may become quacks in many other kinds of business beside that. Our duty is in all business to be true and just, and do our work as just men should.

We must remember, also, that it is not altogether true that riches confer happiness on their possessor. Happiness comes from inward and not outward possessions.

The late Stephen Girard, of Philadelphia, when surrounded with immense wealth, and supposed to be taking supreme delight in its accumulation, wrote thus to a friend:

"As to myself, I live like a galley slave, constantly occupied, and often passing the night without sleeping. I am wrapped up in a labyrinth of affairs, and worn out with cares."

2. The acquisition of office does not, I think, constitute the chief end of a young man's endeavors, for though it may be an honorable thing, in a country like ours, to receive the tokens of confidence which our fellow-men thus show us, it is far more honorable to our character that the office seeks us, because we are thought the best to fill it, than that we should seek the office. Then it comes to us from no desire of our own, but rather through a sense of our fitness which pervades the community, and the position becomes full of honor, only because we fill it with manliness. When we are not equal to it, or when we seek it because we are ambitious, or because of the consideration which we think it brings, or because it is a position a little above

the level of life about us, as we think, we do injustice to ourselves, and become objects of contempt rather than of regard.

> "Man, proud man!
> Drest in a little brief authority;
> Most ignorant of what he 's most assured,
> His glassy essence, — like an angry ape,
> Plays such fantastic tricks before high heaven,
> As make the angels weep; who, with our spleens,
> Would all themselves laugh mortal."

But it is not so much the loss of respect in the estimation of others, which too ambitious office-seeking imposes upon us, as it is loss of real manhood to ourselves. As a general rule, I think it will be found that politics, as a business, has ruined more men than it has benefited; for beside the precarious nature of that occupation which depends upon the fickle popular breath for sustenance, there is a manifest loss of self respect in the possession of power which has been acquired by ignoble and contemptible means, by servility to party interests, and a sacrifice of personal independence to fidelity to party obligations. If office comes, let it come because of one's own worth and capacity. If it does not come, let no one long for it or hanker after it. There are many things joined with it which are full of unhappiness, and even misery. Power has its dangers as well as its delights, and its trials as well as its triumphs. How much better faithfully to work and manfully to live, independent of popular applause, caring nothing for popular condemnation and favor, and, by this very independence and this manful life, to secure a popular approval, the approbation of one's own conscience, and the commending favor of God! Even in its best estate power is unsatisfying, because the soul feels that it needs something more for its nutriment than any of the rewards of ambition, though they be the greatest that the earth can afford.

"By Grecian annals it remained untold,
But may be read in Eastern legend old,
How, when great Alexander died, he bade
That his two hands uncovered might be laid
Outside the bier, for men therewith to see —
Men who had seen him in his majesty —
That he had gone the common way of all,
And nothing now his own in death might call;
Nor of the treasures of two empires aught
Within those empty hands unto the grave had brought."

3. A good reputation is a better thing than money or power for a young man to strive for. "A good name," says the Hebrew proverb, "is better than great riches." It is a noble object of search to seek a reputation which shall have no stain upon it, and which shall make one famous in the recollection of men. To be at the head of one's class in whatever calling; to be known as the best mechanic, the most gifted poet, the most eloquent orator, the ablest statesman, is a good thing to possess—nay, it is a great possession. If it

is sought without selfishness, if it is obtained without dishonor, if it is borne with modesty, it becomes something better than reputation, and is the natural outgrowth of character. Character is the main thing, and to be the best man is better than to have the name of it. There are many manufactured reputations. We can not doubt that when we examine the list of famous men. We wonder what has made them famous, when we reflect how weak and poor their manhood is. How many men we find who seem to be constantly itching for notoriety; who seem to think that the world will forget them, unless they make themselves prominent upon every opportunity, and are constantly on the alert to find a place in which they can introduce their flux of words, that attention may be drawn to themselves. It is not well for any young man to look out upon life as only the stage on which he is to play his part, and catch the applauses of his fellows. It is his duty to be true and manly wherever he may be, let applause come or not, as they will. The world is not so near-sighted or so forgetful as it seems. It has a keen eye and a tenacious memory for every true thing that is done and every true word that is spoken, and it will never let die what is worthy to live. It may not do justly at first, but it does not neglect to have justice done at the last. Let no one think that his life is unappreciated, or complain that he is neglected. No man ever will be neglected who gives his fellow-men any thing worth taking care

of, and the very humblest virtue will be preserved as a blessing. It is well, sometimes, that the world may seem to forget, and it may be that a man is so just and true as to be above the world's commendation. When Cato the censor lived, many ignoble persons had statues erected to their memory. To those who expressed their wonder to the virtuous old Roman that he had none, he said, "He would much rather it should be asked why he had not a statue, than why he had one." Yet it must be remembered that a man must be a Cato to say that with becoming truthfulness!

This rich boon of life, with its unnumbered privileges, was not given any man that he might make his manhood subservient to the uses of any worldly pursuit; but that he might, by the opportunities which an earthly life affords, make his manhood true, firm, brave and perfect. Not that he might be rich, or powerful, or famous, but that by the proper use of his money, power and reputation, he might be a useful and true man. He that is the most useful man is the most successful man; who is simply and truly himself; who takes what God gives him and makes the most of it; who fills his life with deeds of beneficence and good, and leaves the world richer and better than he found it. It may be much, it may be little, that he has to give, but the gift shall mark the giver as a genuine and successful man. He may have wealth, and use it as a faithful steward for the good of all human life. He may have none, and yet cause the hearts of many to bless him. He may have power, and exercise it justly for helping the weak and lifting up the feeble. He may be in obscure and humble life, and yet make every day the witness of some generous and heroic self-denial. He may have knowledge, and give it with unsparing hand for the benefit of mankind. He may be unlettered, and yet have a wisdom that is born of Heaven. He may have fame, and it may be so stainless and so irreproachable that it shall be for a perpetual incitement to others for achievement. He may not be known beyond the limits of his own neighborhood, yet be known by every man around him for love and charity and truthfulness. And when it comes to pass that this world is to be left behind, it will have one true life the more whose accomplishments are to be rejoiced in, and whose departure is to be lamented. Amid the dust and toil of life, will remain a memory, fragrant as the morning, to breathe through long years to come. When — as indeed there may be an instance in your own remembrance now — this humble, truthful, manful, generous life is that of a young man, taken away in the flush of his early strength, there is an unfading record left of it, if not on any page of earthly chronicle, certainly on the inmost substance of your own hearts. Who would not rather leave such pleasant memories than enjoy all the worldly successes which a more pretentious life may gain? An English preacher well and truly says: "The honor, fame, respect, obsequious homage that attend worldly great-

ness up to the grave's brink, will not follow it one step beyond. These advantages are not to be despised; but if these be all that, by the toil of our hand, or the sweat of our brow, we have gained, the hour is fast coming when we shall discover that we have labored in vain and spent our strength for naught. But while these pass, there are other things that remain. The world's gains and losses may soon cease to affect us, but not the gratitude or the patience, the kindness or the resignation, they drew forth from our hearts. The world's scenes of business may fade on our sight, the noise of its restless pursuits may fall no more upon our ear, when we pass to meet our God; but not one unselfish thought, not one kind and gentle word, not one act of self-sacrificing love done for Jesus' sake, in the midst of our common work, but will have left an indelible impress on the soul, which will go out with it to its eternal destiny."

III. Having chosen one's business or profession, the young man should strive to ascertain what there really is in it. There is something more than a dull routine of manual or mental labor in every man's work. It has a science. It is based upon eternal principles, and he who does not understand these, but is contented with the simple art of his business, has not learned half his trade. It is a great advantage to a young man to mingle study with work; and he will find, when once he begins, that the objects of study which are connected with his business are almost numberless. Hugh Miller was a stone mason, engaged in early life in quarrying red sandstone, in Scotland, for building purposes. He became a student of this formation, using, for want of better advantages, the light of the fire which was kindled in the rude cabin of his nightly lodging, and by his habits of study became most eminent as a geologist. George Stephenson was, at seventeen years of age, a fireman in an English colliery. He became a student of the properties and capacities of the steam engine, taking to pieces the one which he tended, and putting it together again, that he might understand its construction, and he became the father of the railway system of Europe and America. Not a man that travels by rail but is indebted to the studious perseverance and the perceptive genius of the English engineer. The art of printing is due to the studies of Guttenburg. There are the most numerous illustrations, which show that the progress of the mechanic arts has depended, and still depends upon the studious habits of working men. It is a great mistake to suppose that professional men are the only persons who need to spend their lives in the pursuit of historical, scientific, biographical and other studies. There is no young man before me, in whatever business he may be engaged, who does not absolutely need the influence of study and mental cultivation to make him not only a better man but a better workman; that he may mingle with his every day toil the refining and humanizing influence of culture;

that his work may be the easier for it, and that he may be more skillful and better in every possible direction.

Cicero, in his oration in behalf of the poet Archias, mentions some of the great men of Roman history, and declares that they became great, partly at least on account of their attention to liberal studies. And he goes on to say that even if this result is not obtained, and if "pleasure alone is sought from these studies, this relaxation of mind is most humane and liberal. For while other things belong to certain places and times, these belong to all times and seasons. They nourish youth; they cheer old age; they adorn prosperity; they afford a refuge and solace for adversity. They delight us at home; they do not impede our acts abroad. They are with us in the night; they travel with us; they go into the country with us," and are always and every where a source of the highest satisfaction. We may learn something, I think, from the Roman orator.

There is another most absurd mistake which deserves notice. Some there are who say that laboring men are not to be educated, because they may be educated above their station. God gave to every man a mind and soul, and the gift implies an obligation to cultivate and develop that mind and soul. And God help that man to understand life better who can not, in his foolish pride, see that the station which he fills, who is faithful to his spiritual and intellectual nature, though his hands may be hard with toil, and his face bronzed with exposure, and his frame sturdy through his honest industry, is better and higher than any station in the whole universe, though it be filled with all the comforts of wealth, and the pomps of power, and the delicacies of fashion. Station! Let a man stand upon his own manly integrity, whatever his business may be, and he stands high enough! There is no station that does not demand that the man who is in it should be educated! Every working man should feel that he has always something to learn, and each day should find him better informed than he was on the day preceding.

Why, for the sake of illustration, should not a house carpenter learn to be an architect as well? Let him study to be so, and he will find himself connected with all history, ancient and modern; with all the sciences, too. He would learn how gradually grew ideas of beauty into facts, and the magnificent temple and shrine were raised, not only to give men an opportunity for worship, but to express religious thought and feeling; every aisle the oratory of prayer, every springing arch the aspiration of devotion. Would he be any less a workman for all this? Not at all, but always more of a workman, for then he would find that he was doing something more than driving nails, and hewing timbers, and wearily shoving the plane; that he was giving form to ideas; that he was growing into a love of the beautiful and true, and that every day's labor was aiding in the noiseless but certain work of building up the structure of a manly and noble character! The farmer has a close connection with all that is best in life and that is purest in nature. His daily business puts him into the closest interest with the physical sciences. Botany, geology, chemistry, natural philosophy, astronomy, all belong to agriculture. He has something more to do than to turn the clods of his soil, to sow the seed and gather in the harvest. There is a mental power in his work; and if he rightly understands the science of his business, he will find that in the earth which he looked not for. "The farmer who sits on his plow-beam," says Emerson, "and discovers the remedy for the potato rot, by pains-taking research and experiment, has the right to say to the professor of botany, 'Come down from your chair, I am a better botanist than thou!'" And he would be. And what a man he might become as he walks over the fragrant earth, and finds pleasure and delight in the soft grass, and the delicate flowers, and the genial air, and the blossoming or fruitful trees, and the pure, fresh, breezy winds, laden with health and strength! With the cultivation of his soil would go on the cultivation of himself, and he would be constantly gathering in from the broad acres of his life a harvest of blessed fruits. Independence, manliness, thrift, would grow up, and the science of agriculture would become a part of the noblest of all sciences — the culture of manhood. These are familiar instances, and I take them to show that even the most familiar occupations can be dignified by intelligence and manliness. It is not true, as we sometimes carelessly say, that any body can be a mechanic or farmer. It requires genius, and skill, and superior knowledge, to become eminent in these as in other matters.

What is true of these labors is true of all. Commerce, what a world-wide influence that has! How many and how important faculties it calls into action! It is not the mere buying and selling — the interchange of commodities. It is the interchange of thought, and feelings, and principles. Ships go freighted with somewhat more than merchandize and gold. They carry with them, into all quarters of the globe, liberty, religion, civilization. The little caraval Santa Maria, as she made her way across the unknown sea, three centuries and a half ago, had on board not simply a crew of discontented Spanish sailors, with their high-souled admiral. The destinies of Humanity were in the little hold. And the Mayflower brought in a cargo, the invoice of which has not yet been written! Who shall say that the merchant or the trader really understands his business, when he thinks of it only as the means of increasing his gains, and not as carrying to their completion Providential plans for the welfare of the whole human race? Or that the sailor really navigates his vessel, if he does not think upon the vast interests which Providence has intrusted to his fidelity? The ledger and the log-book contain not the accounts of trade and the vessel's course alone, but, side by side with these, in invisible characters, are kept the accounts of Humanity, and the course of Progressive History! Be not content, then, O young man, with the mere routine and drudgery of your business, but try to understand what really belongs to it as a part of God's great plans of good!

IV. And so learn the responsibility that belongs to business. We can by no means free ourselves from the sanctions that belong to our present life, reaching over it from the life to come. For the right use of what we have, we must ever be responsible; for the skill, the energy, the enterprise, the strength and vigor which belong to our minds and hands, were given us for God's service, and the service of our fellow-men, and not wholly for our own advantage. We must be true, honest, upright, religious in our business, as in every thing else. We must be careful lest worldliness, avarice, and the selfish love of gain, blunt and deaden our moral principles and our religious feelings. We must scorn to do a mean action. We must despise all dishonesty. We must wage unceasing warfare against every form of business iniquity. How feeble and false the plea which a man raises to excuse his wrong doing, that it is a business transaction, and that he gets his living by it. The slave trader sells human flesh and blood, and speculates in men and women. Of what avail before Him whose clear eye penetrates the flimsiness of human sophistries, and the quibblings of human law, that this is a matter of property and business between man and man? Such property is not recognized at that tribunal, where divine justice holds its court, and the Almighty never yet has given a bill of sale for any human creature! Of what avail the plea of business, when the sorrows of the poor and wronged cry out against him, to that man who fills all social life with wretchedness and crime, and scatters all around him firebrands and death? Shall the man who deals in intemperance and the woes it brings, be shielded by the cry of business and property? Do not say that these are extreme cases! All cases are subject to the same law. Injustice, falsehood, wrong can not be allowed in any business, and there is no act of work that a man may do which is exempt from the principles of equity and right. And this, not because honesty is the best policy in the long run, but because honesty is manly and just, and because there is nothing in all the universe which can serve the stead of truth!

What I have said in relation to business applies equally well to professional life. There, too, are needed industry; a thorough understanding of one's calling, and a complete fitness for it; manliness, truth, honesty and an upright life. If professional men are the leaders of thought and action, it is especially necessary that they should be true, firm, brave and generous; stooping to no false or ignoble action; having a generous sympathy with all humane movements; earnest, independent, liberal and free; working with all their powers, and using all their gifts in the service of truth and human good. Says Lord Bacon: "He that seeketh to be eminent among able men hath a great task; but that is ever good for the public. But he that plots to be the only figure among ciphers, is the decay of a whole age. Honor hath three things in it—the vantage-ground to do good, the approach to kings and principal persons, and the raising of a man's own fortunes. He that hath the best of these intentions when he aspireth is an honest man."

I feel that I am hardly nearer the conclusion of my address than when I commenced it, so numerous are the connections of the subject with human life. But the time warns me not to weary your patience farther. There is but a single point more which I touch, because I can not pass it by. It is the relation of business to growth of character. Side by side, and in intimate union, are each man's daily toil and his spiritual advancement. The school of labor is educating us unto eternal results of good or ill, and our daily, familiar experiences are indications of our manhood. We are producing spiritual as well as material things. The manufacturer is weaving a texture to endure when all mechanical products are forgotten, and has to do with the warp and woof of an eternal life. The mechanic is building a structure which shall outlast the stars. The agriculturist has no farm so broad as that, on which he sows the daily virtue or the daily sin. The merchant is extending his commerce into regions remoter than the farthest corner of the earth, and has intercourse with a world beyond the skies. The sailor is navigating a sea more dangerous than any he has yet sailed over, and is embarked upon a voyage whose haven of destination has a name not down on any of his charts; while the man of thought and study is at school to solve the great problems for which the sciences of numbers furnish no rules. All perception, all action, all life, is converted into character, and no hour passes which does not add to or diminish the depth and power of our moral being.

Let us then go to all our various work, with the assurance that it is for the constant unfolding of Providential plans, and that we are laboring together with God. Let us feel that every hour passed in honest, faithful toil, in counting-house and ware-room, in mill and workshop, over all the land and all the sea — no act lost, and none ineffectual in whatever station, since all stations belong to humanity — is so much accomplished for the real advancement of mankind. It is not merely the products of his skill and work that the faithful man is gathering to himself, but a better product with them — a noble manhood, to cheer and bless all human life. He who fails in doing that, though he may be successful, as men generally count success, is really bankrupt at the last, and dies in that saddest insolvency, where one owes a debt he can not pay to humanity and God!

"O rich man's son! There is a toil,
That with all others level stands;

Large charity doth never soil,
  But only whiten soft, white hands ;
  This is the best crop from thy lands ;
A heritage, it seems to me,
Worth being rich to hold in fee.

" O poor man's son ! scorn not thy state,
  There is worse weariness than thine,
In merely being rich and great ;
  Toil only gives the soul to shine,
  And makes rest fragrant and benign ;
A heritage, it seems to me,
Worth being poor to hold in fee.

" Both, heirs to some six feet of sod,
  Are equal in the earth at last ;
Both, children of the same dear God,
  Prove title to your heirship vast,
  By record of a well-filled past :
A heritage, it seems to me,
Well worth a life to hold in fee !"

V. CONVERSATION—READING—AMUSEMENTS.

In every man's life there are many things which, though manifestly belonging to his life, are yet in a measure separate from its active courses. They are not particularly prominent, yet they never cease to affect the whole course of thought and action; and though they belong more to private experience than to public history, are yet by no means uninfluential in the formation of habits and character. On the contrary, they are especially powerful in their influence, and sometimes sway the whole course of life. In a series of Lectures like this, I could not pass over the subjects which I have announced for this evening in silence. I could have wished to devote more time to their separate consideration, had the limits of the course permitted. I am compelled, somewhat against my will, to combine them, hoping to find a line of unity connecting them with each other, and with the train of thought which we have hitherto pursued.

The first part of this evening's address will be devoted to a consideration of the subject of Conversation. You say this is very common-place. So it is.

So has all been that I have said until now. So it will be to the end. My object has been to be just as common-place as it is possible to be. For it is these very common-place and familiar things which enter most largely into our practical life, and in regard to which it is necessary that we should think clearly and act justly. I think, too, we ought to understand that it is by fidelity to the familiar and common-place affairs of life that we arrive at success in the greatest and most important matters; and thus the familiarity and seeming triviality of our subject give it all the more interest to us, as we are now endeavoring to ascertain how to lead a manful and honest life.

Without question, much of the happiness or grief of life arises from the character of our social intercourse. The gift of speech is a great blessing to us; how great we may not understand till we become deprived of it; and, like all other blessings, it may be abused and become a curse. By it, we communicate our thoughts and feelings to one another, and we could not well be deprived of the intercourse of friendship, the social converse, and the kindly, cheerful talk which we enjoy. We show ourselves, we see others in words; in the tones of voice with which they are spoken, and the spirit that breathes through them. If a man's words to us, as we meet him at our homes or in the street, are hearty, cheerful, manly, full of good and truthful spirit, he challenges and receives our respect and confidence. If his language is coarse, mean, low, vile and false, we are repelled from him, and shun his society. We are strengthened by a free and full communion of thought with a frank, generous, and honest man. We feel weakened and degraded by our companionship with a false, and wicked, and dishonest man. The relief given us is like escaping from a dark and narrow cavern into the free, and fresh, and open sunlight. There are some men that drive us into ourselves, and shut up all the avenues of communication. We can not answer them except by monosyllables, and we wish that the interview was over, that their departure may relieve us of the pressure which they impose upon us. There are other men who draw us out almost involuntarily on our part, and we are surprised, as we remember how open we have been in our conversation and confidence. How often does it happen, too, that a conversation with friends is full of the most delightful enjoyment to us, though the words spoken may be few and feeble. Even the commonest word from those we love is better for us, and does more to encourage and help us, than a stranger's wisest speech! It has been well said by an English writer: "One could take a book from his shelf ten times more wise and witty than almost any man's conversation. Bacon is wiser, Swift more humorous, than any person one is likely to meet with. But they can not chime in with the exact frame of thought in which we happen to take them down from our shelves. Therein lies the luxury of conversation; and when a living speaker does not yield us that luxury, he becomes only a book, standing on two legs." I presume we have all met with persons who talk as though they were thinking how their words would appear in print. Then we have to confess, that however intelligent and even learned their conversation may be, it is still wearisome and uninteresting, because it does not chime in with our thoughts, and also because the persons talking are thinking not so much of us as their own importance, and for all purposes might as well be talking to themselves.

Conversation, however, is something more than a luxury. The voice we have, and the manner in which we use it, is a powerful instrument for good or evil. So it becomes a duty with us to make our conversation not only agreeable for purposes of pleasure, but instructive as an influence of good to others. Every man has something to communicate to his fellow-man, beside needless information about the weather, the state of the money-market, or the trifling gossip that floats about the neighborhood. So our conversation should have for its object the promotion of the welfare of those with whom we talk. It should be filled with truth, with kindness, with encouragement, with consolation. Thus filled, it becomes an important influence which we exert upon all social life, as we confer a benefit upon the whole community when we free our social intercourse from all vicious and false things, and make it full of all good and true things. "A word fitly spoken," says the proverb, "is like apples of gold in pictures of silver;" and there is no one of us so humble and poor but may make another's life happier by some kind and cheerful word. Scientific men tell us that every sound upon the surface of our own and other planets circulates in endless and ceaseless waves through the infinite space. Certainly not less subtle is the influence of our words upon the life and character of the world.

But, say some, talking is of little good; action is the main thing. You say of a man, that he is "all talk." True, there are just such men; men of great wind; who "speak great swelling words of vanity, and are puffed up by their own conceits; wells without water, and clouds carried by a tempest." These are false and foolish men. But there are true men, who sway the world by the influence of speech. The gifted orator moves the multitude at will. Who shall gainsay his power? The quiet fireside discussion, what a power it has over the life! In the early times of conflict in which the Republic was born, who shall say that the eloquence of Otis, and Adams, and Henry, or the quiet, earnest and resolute conversation in patriot homes, did not conduce as much to our triumph, as the actions of Gates, and Greene, and Washington, on the battle-field? And now there are men, whose instruments are mainly words, and who by them are moulding public opinion and educating a people fit to make a state!

Such being the power of words, it becomes a question of some importance as to how we shall regulate that sometimes unruly member, the tongue.

I. What shall be avoided?

1. Thoughtless and idle words. I suppose that much harm is done by thoughtlessness. We are not careful enough in what we say, and words will slip from us sometimes which we would give worlds to recall. We need to think before we speak, lest by our thoughtlessness, our spoken word becomes the master of our lives. There are some proverbs which in their sententious wisdom speak volumes to us; such as that English maxim: "He that says what he likes, shall hear what he does not like." Or perhaps the thought is better expressed by the Spanish proverb: "The evil which isues from thy mouth falls into thy bosom." And the Chinese have a saying which shows us that we make ourselves partakers in the thoughtless words of others: "He who laughs at an impertinence makes himself its accomplice." And there is a Persian proverb, which it would be well for young men and women to remember in concert rooms, lecture halls, and the like; "Speech is silvern, silence is golden." You should remember that the majority of the audience go for the purpose of hearing the speaker or the performer, and not you, and it is particularly impertinent and offensive to disturb them by any thoughtless, impolite, and ridiculous behavior. There is a great deal of heedless gossip, too, which is to be avoided. No community would wish to be

known as scandal-mongers, and the conversation which is made up of detraction, calumny and slander, is especially injurious. Have we not something else to talk about but a neighbor's weaknesses?

2. Cruel and unkind words are not to be spoken. We should not wish to cherish ungenerous and unkind thoughts of any person; much less would we give these thoughts expression. Wounds are inflicted so, that are impossible of cure, and will rankle for years, producing misery and pain. Of this character is the habit of sneering, which is most unlovely in woman and ugly in man, and is evermore to be avoided by all who would be generous and frank. We must try to think the best of every one we meet, and to speak to him or her in a kind and considerate way, remembering that the rudest nature is susceptible to kindness, and may be wounded by a harsh word from us; while we certainly would not be so cruel as to pierce a sensitive soul by our selfish and cutting speech. We must remember that we can injure by our tongue as much as by our hand, and the violence of language may be as harmful as the violence of action.

3. Profane and obscene words are to be avoided. Lewdness of speech is an indication of impurity of soul, and profanity is as vulgar as it is irreverent. Such words are always unchaste, indelicate, improper, and ungentlemanly. Nay, worse than these, they are really vicious; for they have a reflex influence upon the mind and soul, and degrade and weaken the character.

They are demoralizing in their effects, as they are immoral in their character. Let no young man ever allow his tongue to be polluted in this filthy way. Oaths and impurity do not become lips which have been formed in beauty by their Creator to utter words of blessing and good. He that really feels what his language expresses, must have lost all reverence for what is best and purest; while he whose words involuntarily and habitually shape themselves into such forms, must have a hardened heart and a vicious soul. The habit is coarse and disgusting; ungentlemanly, too, as every thing low and disgusting is, and wicked and wrong in all its various aspects. By all means, let it be avoided!

II. 1. On the other hand, conversation should be free, generous, manly, honest, and truthful. What we have to say must be said truthfully; for truth here is as much a duty as elsewhere, and he that is false and dissembling in his words will generally be found false in every thing. The man of faithless and dishonest speech, who conceals the truth, or utters it so as to make it equivalent to falsehood, deserves from us nothing but contempt. The demagogue in public is a despicable man. But there are men of the same character, who never mount the platform, and may not emerge from private life; men of no independence of character, and no moral courage, and full of lies to themselves and all men around them, and if possible to God! Have we a true word to say? let us say it without reserve and freely; say it earnestly, say it lovingly, but say it faithfully! If it shall do good to any human soul, let it go forth, and it shall bear a blessing on its wings; and when it is gone let us be faithful to it, for it is a pledge given by us to the world, which we should be careful to redeem. So when a promise is made, if made in good faith and with full knowledge of its influence, it must be kept and faithfully fulfilled. We sometimes say of an honest man, as though it were creditable to him, "His word is as good as his bond." Is it not discreditable to any man, that his bond should be better than his word? So we take oaths in courts of justice to tell the truth. We do not always remember that we are continually on oath before a tribunal higher than any earthly court; on oath to tell the truth, before the tribunal of our own conscience and our God. I know that we do not always think in this way. I know that the young man, as he goes out into life, expecting truth, uprightness, patriotism, is wofully disappointed. I know how he finds deceit in social intercourse, dishonesty in business, mean and low intrigue for office in politics. I know how soon his high sense of honor is degraded, as he sees, even in the very loftiest positions, falseness and contempt for pledges and professions; sycophancy instead of independence; meanness instead of generosity; hypocrisy instead of religion; how soon he learns the maxims of the world. How soon he falls in with the ways of the hour; how soon he becomes as mean and false and dishonest as the rest! How grand and noble it is, when he remains faithful among the faithless; resolved, come what may — poverty or wealth, reputation or obscurity, success or defeat — there shall be at least one true man!

2. Conversation should be cheerful. What contributes most to the happiness of home is the cheerfulness which fills the little offices of kindness that belong to it. Fretfulness and ill-humor always are destructive to that calmness of enjoyment which makes home the best place in all the world. A passionate, scolding woman is certainly no very pleasant companion for any one. A morose, sullen, angry man is certainly no pleasanter. If such persons are not companionable at home, they would not be very likely to be so abroad. What gives zest and relish to our social enjoyments is the cheerful spirit which fills the observance of the little things, that constitute the charm of social life. How are we drawn to the man whose words are full of cheerfulness! His conversation may not be instructive; he may say nothing but the most common-place things; he may not be witty or brilliant; but every word may be thoroughly brightened by the cheerful spirit which shines through it. It is not so much what he says, as the manner in which he says it; and we bask in his kindly smile and his genial, sunshiny companionship, as we lie on grassy banks on a summer's day, and fill ourselves with joy.

3. Conversation should be religious. By this I do not

mean that unmeaning and insincere cant, which sometimes passes for religious conversation, and which is as husks to the hungry soul. It is not necessary to say specifically religious words, or frame our sentences into religious forms; but there may be a religious spirit of charity and love — love for God, and man, and every thing just and true — which shall breathe through every word, and be the soul of every sentence. When you go into the woods, the sweetest fragrance comes from the delicate and invisible flowers that hide among the underbrush or beneath the leaves, and in social intercourse there may be a spirit, unseen and hiding itself away, and yet be the quickening and animating beauty to every look and all the speech. Religious speech is not always solemn and serious, but may be full of all cheerfulness and gentle ways, and devotion itself may take upon it such a character and aspect of good.

> "To worship rightly is to love each other;
> Each smile a hymn, each kindly deed a prayer!"

II. Leaving now the conversation by the living voice, we come to the conversation on a higher plane, viz., with books — READING.

It has been said that a man is known by the company he keeps. I think he may be better known by the books he reads. He may sometimes be thrown into company which he does not select for himself, but his books are matters of choice. So prolific is the press in our day, and so inexpensive are its products, that every one has the widest choice of the best books; every taste may be gratified, and every shade of thought finds ample opportunity for expression. Nothing is so abundant as are books. "Consider," says Emerson, "what you have in the smallest chosen library. A company of the wisest and wittiest men that could be picked out of all civilized countries, in a thousand years, have set in best order the results of their learning and wisdom. The men themselves were hid, inaccessible, solitary, impatient of interruption, fenced by etiquette; but the thought which they did not uncover to their bosom friend is here written out in transparent words to us, the strangers of another age."

Think what an influence books have and exert! Bad books are mischievous in the extreme, for they excite the worst part of our natures, and make our life, while reading them, shameful and wicked. We may be ashamed to be seen in company with a bad man, but we allow ourselves to read his book almost without compunction. The influence is invisible, and it may even be imperceptible, but it is insidious and sure. We may be unable to see the danger which lies concealed beneath the surface, and, almost before one is aware, the character may be corrupted and the structure of manhood undermined. This is particularly the case with the young; for at the ductile time of life when habits are forming, and character is grow ing, a corrupt book may lead into ways of wrong, and sin, and vice, filled with a lifelong misery. We regard as a murderer, and justly so, the man who puts poison into the food which we use for the nourishment of the body; but what shall we call the man who poisons the food which we take for the nourishment of the mind and soul? And we, ourselves, become moral suicides if we take the poison that is offered.

On the other hand, who can estimate the influencé of a good book? It is as though we were admitted into the familiar intimacy with a wise and good man, who talks to us with all confidence and friendship. His intercourse with us soothes, encourages, inspires us. Conversation with books, says Montaigne, "goes side by side with me in my whole course, and every where is assisting me; it comforts me in age and solitude; it eases me of a troublesome weight of idleness, and delivers me at all hours from company that I dislike; and it blunts the point of griefs, if they are not extreme." We know how true this is, and how the books of good and true men come to us with their "medicine for the mind." What society in solitude! What comfort in pain and grief! What a high and holy friendship with the most gifted minds of the world! They share their best thoughts with us; they tell us of their joys and sorrows; they introduce us into the experience of life, and show us what we ourselves are, so that he who has a well chosen library, though it be not above a hundred volumes, has, in his own home, beneath his own roof-tree, and at his own fireside, the poet, the historian, the scholar, the philosopher, the wide traveler, the deepest thinker; and with them all may hold the sweetest converse, as the dearest friends, and learn of them how to live, and be a man. Who that has Milton, Shakspeare, Plato, Socrates, and the best writers of the age, for his daily companions can be mean, and base, and unworthy? How can he be otherwise than brave and noble? "Books," says an old English writer, "are the masters who instruct us without rods and ferules, without hard words and anger, without clothes or money. If you approach them, they are not asleep; if investigating, you interrogate them, they conceal nothing; if you mistake them, they never grumble; if you are ignorant, they never laugh at you."

Books have two uses for us. They serve either as a relaxation from our severe physical toils, giving us the pleasures which belong to intellectual activity, or they become to us the means of self-improvement. There are few men whose occupations are such as wholly to deprive them of the opportunity of reading. There is no young man who can not find time for improving himself in this way. Even a single hour, thus spent each day, will be found to amount to a vast deal in a lifetime, and will be the means of instruction hardly appreciable by those who have not made the experiment. One would be astonished to find how great an accumulation of the most useful and gratifying knowledge might thus be made, and how valuable would be such a furniture of the mind. Sir Edward Lytton Bulwer, one of the most active of the literary men in our times, the author of numerous books of fiction, and a man of great learning, is said to have spent but three hours each day in reading, writing and study; but during these three hours he paid the closest attention to his work. In a country like ours, it is impossible for any one to say what position he will be called upon to fill. It is needful that each one qualify himself to fill it worthily. A very little time saved each day from places of idle resort, or from hours of indolence, and spent in useful reading, would suffice to fit young men for almost any station in life. It is also for the utmost advantage for every one to pursue a line of study a little apart from his daily toil. Instances are by no means wanting of courses of study pursued by working men, who have, by diligent husbandry of time, become eminent in their calling, and in whatever position the circumstances of their after life may have placed them. Franklin, a man of great industry, found time, amid the plays of boyhood and the toils of manly life, to read. He was a student from his very infancy. A tallow-chandler and a printer, he yet did not neglect the cultivation of his mind, nor think that because he was a working man he did not need the fruits of study. The candle, which possibly he had moulded himself, furnished him the light he needed in his little garret, for perusing some well worn volume, into the small hours of the night. The habits of early life never forsook him, and he was always a student. He was a working-man by necessity. He was a student by choice, and his study and work never clashed with each other. He was no less studious because he was a workman, and he was no less industrious because he was a student. Robert Burns was a poor plowman in Scotland. He tells us that his verses were generally composed in the fields, while he was at work upon the various labors of the farm, and afterward transcribed at home. But he was no less good as a farmer because he was so glorious a poet. Nor was Hugh Miller less faithful in the stone quarry, because he was learning to be a geologist. We ought to understand that this intellectual and spiritual nature, which is so active beneath the surface of our working life, craves its food as much as the physical nature which we have. The arm is no less brawny, the hand no less strong, the fingers no less skillful, because the mind has its proper aliment, and grows strong day by day by what it feeds upon. And we ought also to bear in mind that the cultivation of this nature has a tendency "to refine the work-day life and adorn it; to disengage it from the contacts of matter;" to elevate it to a connection with ideas, truths and principles, and fill it with objects of beauty and of love. Is there any young man who complains of a want of time or opportunity? If he has no money to buy books of his own, there are libraries to which he can have ready access, and there is no young man who can not find both time and opportunity to improve them, if he only has the inclination. It is an excellent practice for a young man to select some subject and write upon it, that he may learn to think and express his thoughts with clearness and correctness. Thus he makes his reading useful to some good end. It may be difficult, but it will be found exceedingly serviceable; and in our community the facilities for both reading and writing are so numerous that the young man is blamable if he does not use them.

But you ask, What shall we read? First, I answer, read the best books which you can find upon the subjects to which your inclination or desire for improvement leads you. If possible, never read a poor book upon any subject. You can soon find, generally in the first few pages, whether the book helps or inspires you, and whether the author has any soul in him, or only the semblance of one. If there is any exhibition of insincerity or a desire to write for effect, or attempts at fine composition, without regard to the vigor and purity of thought, the book is better let alone. Your time can be better employed. This rule, I think, is worth following in regard to works of fiction and poetry. Those are to be read which belong to the first rank in their respective class. I am very far from indulging in an indiscriminate abuse of novel reading, because I think that no one's reading is complete which does not embrace this. The creations of the imagination are necessary and beneficial to be understood. We do not find our happiness and good in continually remaining in the practical, prosaic world. We need sometimes to go out of ourselves into the ideal world of poet and dramatist, and the writer of fiction. The imagination is an important faculty of our nature, and every young man should cultivate it. It is well for us to rise above our daily toil, and rejoice in the beauty and gladness which the imagination creates. Fiction is not necessarily false, because it is fictitious. It has been used many times for the purpose of illustrating and enforcing the best truth. Our childhood's reading is mostly of a fictitious kind, and yet we are seldom the worse for it. The parables of the New Testament are fictitious, although they are far from being untrue; and there was many a precept which Jesus gave under the form of a parable, that became more forceful by the garb with which his imagination clothed it. In our day the novel is made the vehicle of philosophy and religion, and many an abuse and many a falsehood receive their death blow from the genial humor of Dickens, and the pungent satire of Thackeray. I think we have much to be grateful for, and indeed there is a gratifying indication of progress, in the fact that the tone of our fiction is generally so manly and true. The taste of the people is improving. We are learning to read rightly and well, and no book can pass current among us, or enjoy any extended circulation, unless it has the ring of the true metal in it. I do not know that I need to mention what authors are to be read in this department. The two whom I have just referred to, Scott, and Bulwer in his later works, our own countrymen, Cooper and Irving, the old English poets, dramatists and writers, Shakspeare and his cotemporaries, Addison, with his associates, Goldsmith, and the galaxy of literary men who adorned his times, Charles Lamb, with his coterie of friends, are by no means unworthy of the young man's attention. To these may be added a few female writers of our own day, like Mary Howitt, Charlotte Brontë, Mrs. Gaskell, Miss Martineau, in her earlier and better years, and Mrs. Stowe, whose large humanity gives them claims to our regard. The young man and woman who makes the acquaintance of these noble men and high-souled women, will not be satisfied with those namby-pamby and flimsy love stories, desecrating the noble passion by their feeble imitation, which I am glad to feel are passing out of existence. They are fit for only love-sick damsels and swains, who make the heroes and heroines —save the mark!—of these novels the representatives of their own cases. But, as love-sickness is a kind of disease similar to those which sometimes attack children, and generally as harmless; and to which perhaps we are all more or less exposed, it is to be hoped that the popularity of these books will be as evanescent as the feeling that gives them interest.

2. There is a better kind of reading than that of fiction. Biography and history should never be neglected

by a young man. When we read the biographies of noble men we are introduced at once into the society of heroes, and the earth is better and more sacred to us, because it has borne such grand and honorable persons. We need to know how human life has been carried on in the past. We need to see how the volume of time has rolled through the ages, and what it has carried upon its surface, and in its depths; how God has revealed himself through the life of men. We need to see, too, how the same great capacities have dwelt in the human soul through all the centuries of its life; that it has been swayed by the same passions; that it has been moved by the same aspirations; that it has been carried forward through the same struggles, and gained the same victories by the same unwearied fidelity. Whether beneath an Oriental or an Occidental sun; whether on the banks of the Ganges, along the shores of the Jordan and the Nile, or where our Western waters roll their course to either sea; there have been the same human nature and the same human life. People and empires rise, and fall, and die. The wave of oblivion may sweep away some of the ancient landmarks of the race, but the line of continuity remains unbroken, and the truth of the unity of mankind declares itself through all past and present time! Let the young man then study history; particularly that part which is called the essence of history, the biography of those men whose lives have made history, with the hope, as Carlyle says, "of gaining some acquaintance with our fellow-creatures — though dead and vanished, still dear to us; how they got along in those old days, suffering and doing; to what extent and under what circumstances they resisted the devil and triumphed over him, or struck their colors, and were trodden under foot by him; how, in short, the perennial battle went, which men call life, which we also, in these new days, with indifferent fortune, have to fight, and must bequeath to our sons and daughters to go on fighting, till the enemy be one day vanquished and abolished, or the great night come down and separate the combatants." Shall not the examples which the men of old have set before us, as they fought the enemy and conquered, inspire us to fight the good fight, and achieve the victory as faithfully and as gloriously as they did? We may inherit their valor and their gentleness. We may emulate their bravery and their generosity. We may surpass them, if we will, in manly heroism.

"I know not that the men of old
  Were better than men now,
Of heart more kind, of hand more bold,
  Of more ingenuous brow;
I heed not those who pine for force
  A ghost of Time to raise,
As if they thus could check the course
  Of these appointed days.

Still, it is true, and over true,
  That I delight to close
This book of life, self-wise and new,
  And let my thoughts repose

On all that humble happiness
  The world has since foregone —
The daylight of contentedness
  That on those faces shone!"

So far as the young man of our day can do, he ought to enter into the exploration of the vast field of study, which lies open in the biography of those who have been the heroes of the race. I think there is scarcely a more fascinating book in this respect than Plutarch's Lives. The Christian Fathers, too, have a biography well worth studying. The founders of religion, like Mahomet — the great men of the Papal Church, like Hildebrand — the Reformers of the sixteenth century, like Luther, shaking the world by the force of liberty and truth — are all necessary to be known; while no young American should be ignorant of the lives of those men of our own history whose heroism is the birthright of us all — Washington and his compatriots — the old Puritans and the Fathers of New-England; of old England's worthies too, for English history belongs to us as well as our own — Cromwell — Hampden — the Sydneys — Milton — Howard, and such women as Elizabeth Fry, and those others whom I have already mentioned, and many more,

"Not widely known, but widely blessing human life."

I mention these English books, because, as a general thing, we have not time to go beyond an understanding of our own tongue, and because, too, that brave old English-Saxon speech is the best for us to learn. It may be rugged, it may be rude, it may want the flexibility of other languages, but it is our mother-tongue — spoken by dear friends now in heaven — spoken by the noblest men that ever lived; and it is a manly tongue, a grand and noble language. Let us never be unfaithful to its service. If we have time, indeed, we should extend our knowledge, that we may read the masterpieces of classic times, and the beautiful productions of other climes; but we must be faithful to our own speech first!

3. The young man should read science and philosophy, that he may understand how the great facts of the earth's life have come to be what they are, and how human life is carried on and by what principles. He may not become a philosopher or a scientific man, but he ought to investigate thoroughly and think correctly.

4. There is, too, one book which the young man ought never to neglect, and that is the grand old book — the Bible. This should be his guide, his counsellor, his friend. It contains poetry, romance, history, biography, philosophy, all of the very highest kind, and no one has learned of life and its great aims, unless he has studied the Bible earnestly and reverently. The profound wisdom of those old Hebrew sages — the words of Christ — the Apostles' wondrous speech, as with cloven tongues — we can not afford to lose the inspiration which their teachings

give. All things are there that he needs — help in temptation, encouragement in duty, consolation in sorrow, cheering words in difficulty, and a stay in all his weakness. Through present dangers, and through present joys, this Book of books leads him with safe and glad step, and at the last, when the shadows of death are closing round his way, it shows him the light of eternal glory which beams beyond the tomb! Young man! never neglect the reading of the Bible! Take that book as the lamp of your feet, the guide of all your way. You will find that it does not lead you wrong. Its paths are by the side of still waters, and in the green pastures of a Divine Love!

III. I am obliged to touch lightly upon the third part of this Address, or to risk the wearying of your patience. Still, I can not but think that the subject of Amusements is one of the most important which we shall consider in our whole course of thought. It is a much more serious question than we are apt to suppose, what are suitable amusements for a young man. How shall he employ his hours of recreation? They may be so employed as to leave behind them the sting of unavailing regrets for misspent time, or those feelings of satisfaction which belong to the substantial pleasures of moral and intellectual enjoyment.

Certainly the necessity of recreation of some kind is apparent. It would be useless for me to attempt to show that the young demand amusement. God made us not altogether for serious employment. We were not created wholly for toilsome work, useful as it may be for the development of our faculties. We have no right, in the provision which we make for mental and religious education, to push aside those portions of our being which require play for their complete growth and maturity. It is as much a part of our lives to give occasion and opportunity to ourselves for enjoyment, as it is to make ourselves useful. Nay, we may be as useful in making others happy, as in supplying their necessities. It is as imperative on a Christian community to furnish proper amusements, as it is to furnish religious instruction. Well arranged gymnastic exercises are fully as important to every school-house, as proper accommodations for study and recitation.

Taking human nature as we find it, and as God in his infinite wisdom saw fit to create it, it is more the work of the Christian thinker to try to discover the true relation between the work and play of life, and unite them in an harmonious whole, than to condemn the play of life as altogether irreligious and sinful, and by all means to be avoided. Here is the simple fact, that man has the playful element in his nature which will express itself in some way, either innocently or harmfully. If those amusements which are harmless fall under condemnation, those which are injurious will certainly be found. Then there will be one of three things accomplished—a severe asceticism, utterly crushing all expressions of gay and joyous feeling, with a certain reaction; or a full, unrestrained and defiant course of sensual and debasing pleasures; or a secret pursuit of these pleasures, beneath a hypocritical seeming of rigid propriety. Neither of these can be a beneficial influence upon character. Asceticism is hurtful; gross sensuality is wicked; hypocrisy is worse than both. It has been thought by some that the strict Puritanism of early days has been the prolific source of the license and intemperance of these latter times. Whether this be so or not, this much is unquestionably true, that there is always a force in the human mind which reacts against undue restraint. If the bonds are too tightly fastened they will be broken, and the danger is that the resistance may become insane, and the liberty which is obtained will go beyond itself and become the freest license. We are accustomed to think of ourselves as a nation of plodders, always and feverishly at work, with occasional remissions of toil, when we either express our playfulness in the most unparalleled noise and overwhelming din — as on Independence day — or give ourselves up to the worst indulgences, and call them relaxation and rest, instead of so combining the light with the heavy duties of life in such excellent and harmonious proportion, that each may temper and relieve the other, and both combined produce a full, rounded, and complete character.

For the sake of convenience, I class amusements as follows: 1. Those which are positively injurious. 2. Those which are innocent in themselves, but liable to abuse. 3. Those which are innocent and beneficial.

1. Amusements which are positively injurious. They are, in general, those which stimulate our worst passions and appetites. Whatever helps the evil within us to overcome the good, weakens the power of our moral convictions and undermines our religious principles, is harmful to us. What was begun as a relaxation becomes a vice, and allying itself with its kindred vices, makes the last state of the man worse than the first. Such is gambling in its various forms. There is, without doubt, a pleasurable excitement in gaming. There may be some mental exercise too. But when we think of its demoralizing influence upon the character, and the disgraceful end to which it directly leads, we are furnished with an inducement which would cause us to avoid exposure to its fascination. Never does any course of conduct lead more directly to misery and woe, the destruction of all true happiness, and the vitiation of all manly energy. Little by little is its victim drawn by its allurements within the charmed circle of its influence. Like the fabled mäelstrom, its outer circle may move slowly and weakly. But within that is a narrower, and stronger and swifter; and within that a stronger and swifter still, till at last in the vortex of the whirlpool, the waters rush down with irresistible force. A gallant ship, with rich freight of passengers and merchandize, by the negligence or boldness of her commander, is steered within the influence of the current. Suffered to go too far, she is driven with resistless power. Her sails may be full. Favor-

able winds may be blowing. The man who walks her quarter-deck may have no equal in the art of navigation. But she will not answer to her helm. Not the strength of her timbers, not the value of her cargo, not the character of her passengers, not the skill of her master can be now of any avail, and she is hurried into the abyss amid cries of agony and despair. It is but a feeble picture of the danger into which the young man falls who trusts himself to this most terrible temptation. Playing for small sums leads to playing for large ones. The game is seductive. Nights are sleeplessly spent. Daily business is neglected. Family and friends are deserted, and absolute ruin is in the prospect. The apprentice, the clerk or the student is soon debauched; finds his wages or his allowance insufficient to support such an extravagant amusement; is tempted to defraud his employer, or guardian; yields to the temptation; theft, dishonesty, perhaps forgery, crime follows; small sins lead to great ones, and if the prison or the penitentiary is escaped, it is only by some fortunate combination of circumstances. But be assured the man can not escape from himself. His consciousness of iniquity goes with him, and there is no foreign country and no community of strangers which can afford an asylum for the man who is driven round the world by the goadings of an evil conscience, and the fear of detection and exposure of his guilt. The mechanic, the business or the professional man, is equally subject to such temptation; the danger is equal, the result is similar. Then, too, the gambling-house is always next door to the drinking room, and next the brothel, and next the jail, and next the gallows, and next the dread realities of Eternity! Step by step, each leads to the other! By a singular felicity of expression, gambling-houses are called HELLS. It is the appropriate name. Is a young man safe within their walls?

What I have said respecting this matter, applies equally well to betting at horse races and elections, lottery selling and buying, gambling in fancy stocks, and other similar proceedings. They all lead to the neglect of business, the desertion of home, fraud, depravation of character, the poisoning of life, the debasement of manhood. All sensual pleasures are of the same class. The ruin of manly virtue and of womanly beauty, by what has been called "the crime of great cities," belongs with these. They are not properly amusements. They are vices, and vice is always ruinous. As I write this address, I have before me the account of a man,* once an eminent politician, well descended, educated and honored; a member of the New-York State Constitutional Convention, and a candidate of a powerful party for the office of Secretary of State, he had every inducement to keep true to the line of integrity. But the account goes on to say, "He gave way to a passion for gaming, became involved, and undertook to extricate himself by raising

* James C. Forsyth.

money with the forged signatures of his father and his father-in-law. Exposed he fled, and was a wanderer over the earth until life became an intolerable burden. He has died ere he has seen forty years, a blasted, ruined man." And of how many might there be made a similar record.

2. I pass to the second class of amusements; those which are innocent in themselves, but are liable to abuse. These are of a social nature, and of a physical and intellectual character. Among these I mention only those which are most common.

Dancing is perhaps the most popular amusement now practiced by the young of both sexes, and enters into every thorough scheme of education. It is a practice common to all ages and countries, and has been used to express various emotions. It has not been deemed unworthy to hold a place among even religious exercises. Among the early Haytiens it partook of a serious and mystic character. In civilized countries it is regarded more in the light of a pastime, and has become a most popular amusement. Under proper regulations, and in a company of friends, it can be pursued not only without injury, but to great physical advantage. The exercise is healthful, the movement graceful, and the excitement pleasurable and harmless. It is accompanied with inspiring music, and belongs even to the domain of art; but it is liable to great abuse, and becomes injurious when accompanied by late hours, insufficient clothing, untimely suppers, and the like. In instances where the vile and the virtuous are mingled indiscriminately, the association of dancing, particularly in the voluptuous waltz, is exceedingly harmful. Many a young woman has sown the seeds of premature disease and death in the heated atmosphere, and many a young man has learned his first lesson in vice among the temptations of the ball-room. Especially should children be saved from all such stimulations. Their health should not be sacrificed, nor their character put in jeopardy by the too indulgent fondness of parents. Precocity is excited by irregularities in this respect; and precocity is particularly dangerous in every possible respect. There should be a wise discrimination exercised in regard to this amusement, and where this is properly exercised there need be little fear for the result. It may degenerate into frivolity, and become little more than foppishness, but it may also be made one of the pleasantest and healthiest of recreations. It is said of Mr. Webster—and there is a moral in the story which I leave with you to discover—that being one evening at a ball, he was asked by a young man present, "Do you dance, Mr. Webster?" "No, sir," replied the statesman, "I never had any capacity for dancing!"

Another popular amusement, and about which there has been much recent discussion, is the Theatre. The drama has always been cherished among cultivated nations, not only as an intellectual recreation of a high order, but also as an intellectual accomplishment of the very highest class. Among all nations the greatest writers have expressed their best thoughts in this form. In the Bible the book of Job has ever been considered as the most profound and grand piece of sacred writing in the Old Testament, and this book is the dramatic book of the Hebrew Scriptures. It is a drama of the very loftiest kind. Among the ancient Hindoos, the drama became the medium of teaching both philosophy and religion. Among the Greeks and Romans the drama was esteemed in exceeding honor, and the gems of classic literature are to be found in the productions of the dramatists belonging to those refined and powerful peoples. Among nations of a later time the drama has held a high position. Modern literature has expended its treasures upon it. Shakspeare is the great poet of human nature, and the great philosopher, too. It has not been, however, because of the dramatic form into which the greatest writers have thrown their thoughts, so much as the substance of the thoughts, which have given the drama its immortality as an intellectual master-piece. It is because something more than amusement has been aimed at, namely, instruction and intellectual excitement.

This being so, it would hardly be supposed that there could arise so strenuous an objection to dramatic representations as our times have developed — not among those least capable of appreciating the excellence of the drama, so much as among the cultivated and scholarly, who know all the power and beauty of its character—unless there was something to justify their censure. Certainly, there could hardly seem to be any more injury in listening to the recital of a play, than in reading it from a book. Certainly, if Shakspeare should occupy so prominent a place in every thoughtful man's library, it would hardly seem just that he should be condemned when he appears upon the boards of a theatre. The objection, therefore, can not be to the drama itself, and no man can make such objection without stultifying himself. It must lie against the manner of its representation. I can hardly think that any one could object to such representation among a party of friends, desirous of pleasing and being pleased, provided the play is well selected and properly performed. There must be, of course, a choice in the plays. There are some productions of this kind, which are neither suitable for reading, or for presentation before a virtuous and intelligent audience. They are low and vulgar in their character, with a more than occasional profanity and obscenity; of feeble wit, presenting foolish views of life, making a mock of the holiest affections of our nature, and the highest institutions of society; disrespectful to woman and unjust to man. And, I think, this is the character of too many of the plays that are put upon the stage. This is the reason why there is so much iniquity connected with the stage; for no person can engage in the performances of such plays without having the purity of their nature corrupted, and their best affections blunted and poisoned by the influence of simulated passions.

This is what makes theatre-going unsatisfactory and injurious. It may be all true that dramatic representations are but pictures of real life. "All the world's a stage, and all the men and women merely players. They have their exits and their entrances. And one man in his time plays many parts." It may be that there are actors in the pulpit and the forum, as well as on the stage, who pretend what they do not feel. It may be that much of the denunciation of the theatre is aimless and unjust. Still, there are many points in which it is open to the gravest censure; for the character of its representations; for the wickedness that finds an uncensured shelter within its walls, and about its purlieus, and for the undoubted harmful influence which it exercises upon its habitual attendants, and the general influence which it exerts upon the community. Let it not be claimed that the theatre is the handmaid and promoter of virtue, for we all know that it is not; that it is the educator of the people, for there are better agencies for such education; that it is the delineator of human nature, the tragedy and comedy of life, for we do not need to go within its walls to witness that. The real tragedy of life — its poverty, wretchedness, misery and woe, which is to be seen daily in all our streets, far exceeds the mimic which is shown in its unmeaning emptiness before the foot-lights of the stage. I very much question the depth of that nature which floods the cheeks with tears before the fictitious sufferings of the theatre, but can look with unmoved countenance and the very dryest eye upon the real sorrow and pain that fill a thousand homes with woe. I know it has been argued that religious men should attend the theatre for the sake of reforming it, and that if the best portion of the community would support it, there would soon be a change for the better. The manager presents the plays which suit the audience. The argument would be equally valid in another direction. It might be, that if the customers of a drinking-shop should only call for a glass of cold water or innocent lemonade, in their daily visits, and be willing to pay the usual price for their tipplings, such an establishment would become, if not a public benefit, a very harmless place of resort. But it by no means follows that you and I should go there and buy the water and the lemonade in order to produce such a result. Let the theatre rest on its own merits or demerits as a place of amusement. It may be made inoffensive, if the public demand that it should be made so. It may become, and, indeed, I think it is now, injurious in many respects. There are other amusements which a young man will find far more beneficial and satisfactory.

3. These, I pass now to consider. They are generally to be found in the open air, and are healthful, physically and morally. The greatest need of our

people now, is of stalwart and strong men, and healthy women. To supply this need we must have more out-of-door recreations. In the winter, skating and coasting are capital exercises for both sexes; through the whole year, horse-back riding, if one can afford the expense; or gymnastic performances of some kind. In the summer, excursions in the woods or on the sea, halcyon days snatched from the dull routine of toil, to rest the body and the mind; communion with nature in her various moods; hunting; fishing; not so much for wanton destruction of life, as for the exercise which they produce, and the acquaintance with nature which they furnish; music, with its charms to soothe and please us — these are all good for us, and least liable to be abused. Manly sports, in the fresh air, are not to be despised or condemned. Could the games of Old England be continued in New-England, they would make us as a people more powerful, more robust and more athletic. "Children's plays," says some one, "are nonsense, but they are very educative nonsense." There is boy enough in almost every man to enable him to enjoy, and profit by even the games of his boyhood. They would be much better for him than some of the amusements in which he indulges; would give him a sounder body and a sounder mind, a fresher and younger heart, and a more generous soul. Could he engage in them without a remembrance or consciousness of his conventional dignity, he would find them very profitable in every manner. How much better to breathe the pure air of the open country than the close and poisoned atmosphere of the ball-room; to enjoy the glorious sunshine, and all the scenes of nature's beauty, and the great life action continually going on, than the paltry daubs of the theatre; to go out into the cool shades of the forest, and the light of warm hillsides, by the side of murmuring brooks and the placid lake, and revel in the calm enjoyment of genial suns and breezy airs, underneath the continually varying beauty of the sky, than to share the excitements of the gaming table and the billiard room, or with vile associates waste the hours in ribaldry and vice!

Izaak Walton, in his charming book, The Complete Angler, says of the influences of nature: "As a pious man advised his friend that to beget mortification he should frequent churches, and view monuments and charnel-houses, and then and there consider how many dead bones time had piled up at the gates of death; so, when I would beget content and increase confidence in the power, and wisdom, and providence of Almighty God, I will walk the meadows, by some gliding stream, and there contemplate the lilies that take no care, and those very many other various little living creatures that are not only created, but fed — man knows not how — by the goodness of the God of Nature, and therefore trust in him."

It is true that among the best scenes some evil may dwell, and young men not satisfied with calm delights seek their excitement in artificial stimulus. I do not understand why a water excursion can not be made without the companionship of spirituous liquors; and it is something for a young man especially to avoid, that he may not contaminate the purity of nature by the indulgence of a selfish appetite.

But in all things we are to remember that our periods of rest and relaxation, whether we spend them in conversation with friends, or in agreeable intercourse of books, or in healthful amusements, are to be used by us for strengthening ourselves for the better performance of the duties of life. Life is not a play. It is a serious work, and our play must be more delightful, that our work may be more faithful and effective. The true secret of enjoyment of any pleasure is moderation and content. Let us be grateful for the many sources of happiness which God has opened. Let us enjoy these with a fresh, and loving, and religious spirit. A true religion never frowns upon any innocent amusement. Nay, a truly religious man finds the purest happiness in such, for he is filled with every thing that can make life blessed, and depending upon himself and God, finds in every scene something to make him happier. Religion has a joy, too, which is never taken from us; the joy of devoted worship of God; the joy of disinterested service to the welfare of our fellow-men. There is no pleasure which earth can afford so satisfying as this. Finally, then, let us so live that our conversation may be as becometh the gospel of Christ; that the book of life which writes down our deeds may be read by us at last with entire satisfaction; and that all our hours may be spent, whether we work or play, to fit us for the unending blessedness of the life hereafter.

> "Alas! our time is here so short,
> That in what state soe'er 't is spent,
> Of joy or woe, does not import,
> Provided it be innocent.
> But we may make it pleasant, too,
> If we will take our measures right,
> And not what Heaven has done, undo
> By an unruly appetite."

VI. THE YOUNG MAN IN THE STATE.

THUS far in our course we have considered to such length as our limits have allowed, the position and duties of a young man in the various conditions of life —at home, in business, and in society. It becomes necessary to consider him in his political relations; to ascertain his connection with his country, and to see what duties grow out of such connection. So our subject, this evening, is Patriotism, or the Young Man in the State.

In a certain degree, the train of our thoughts hitherto has been related to the subject now under consideration. For a genuine patriotism would demand that a young man should be faithful to all individual, family, social and business duties, that he might make the best contribution possible to his country. The faithful, honest, generous and energetic man, building up a good home, remembering his dependence upon others in society, and diligent in his business is conferring a benefit upon his country no less than upon himself. Though this be so, it is still not unprofitable to devote our thoughts more particularly to a subject like this, which brings us in direct contact with one of the noblest human virtues.

We define Patriotism, in general terms, as a love of one's own country. We recognize its existence in the hearts of the people of every clime and every nation. The most sterile regions of the earth, and the most unpromising circumstances can not quench in the hearts of men a love of the land which gave them birth. It is at once their happiness and their pride. It now incites them to heroic action, it now gives to them a consciousness of secure repose; it now fills them with aspirations for their country's highest welfare; it now sends them out to achieve that welfare at the cost of all earthly possessions and good. Now it makes them forget all things for the land they love the best; and now, it leads them with a self-devotion that inspires admiration, to willingly give up life itself, and all that makes life blessed, if their country demands the sacrifice. What the old Latin proverb said, "*Dulce et decorum est pro patriâ mori,*"—Sweet and honorable is it for one's country to die—is the expression of every true man's best feeling. Whatever may be its source, and whatever elements combine to produce it, whether love of home, of neighborhood, of State, community of language or community of interests, or whether there is something deeper than all these, here is the feeling, and I, for one, thank God that he has put it into men's hearts. However poor, or weak, or insignificant one's country may be, still that love does not die out. The Irish emigrant, whose beautiful land has been cursed for ages by cruel oppression on one hand, and fierce and bloody vindictiveness on the other; which God has made so bright, but selfish man has so cruelly darkened over by his sin, never forgets the "old country," to which his hopes return, and in which his memories are buried; where are the graves of his fathers, and where he hopes some day himself to die. The German's eyes are strangely moistened when he thinks of the Fatherland — dear still, though its oppression drove him forth. The bosom of the Hungarian swells with honest pride when he remembers the glories of his country's history, or weeps over her sad fate, as she lies bleeding beneath the tyrant's foot. And France and Italy are held in affectionate remembrance by their exiled sons, though the perfidious usurper holds both within his merciless grasp. The Swiss recounts the story of Tell; the Norwegian and the Swede do not weary in their reminiscence of Northern Skäld and Saga. There can scarcely be a heavier grief — next to that of the bereavement of dear friends — than that which is caused by a forced expatriation. Other lands may be better and more fruitful, may have a brighter sky and a warmer sun, may be filled with more plenty, more happiness, and more of earthly good, but however much may be said of these, there is still no land like the land one calls his own.

Still, notwithstanding the strength and depth of this feeling, it does not express the entire meaning of the word Patriotism. The love of country, merely as such, is a comparatively weak sentiment. There is something stronger and far more profound, and that is, the *love of the idea which the country ought to embody.* The love of what is on the outside is a superficial feeling. That which should engross the soul is the love of what is internal, what gives beauty and vigor to the outward life. When we love a friend, we love the beauty and purity of the inward life, whatever may be the character of the outward condition and circumstances. True love does not join itself to a handsome exterior, but to a beautiful heart; for within the outside beauty there may be an unlovely spirit, while a plain and homely exterior may be the guise of an angelic soul. Just so it is with a genuine patriotism. It is not the love of the country's name, nor of its material greatness, prosperity, or wealth; nor of its rocks and hills, its rivers, lakes, plains, and mountains; nor even of its position among the nations; perhaps not altogether of the grand achievements of its history — but the love of what is pure and true and right and noble in the national life — of what is lovely, great, glorious in the national idea — the love of what is found to be the design which God meant the nation should accomplish. And as no true love concerns itself with fond endearments and professions of attachment and protestations of affection, but in a real desire to accomplish the loved one's good and the real labor for the loved one's benefit, so a real love of country by no means is to be guaged by professions of devotion and patriotism, but is to be known and shown by downright, effective labor for the country's highest good, and an unshaken fidelity to the country's design and idea. If patriotism is to be measured by words, the most wily politician is the purest patriot. It is easy to make professions; but he that manfully and modestly labors where God has placed him for the country's good, is more effectual than a host of ambitious, time-serving, venal politicians, who only flatter the prejudices of the people in order to betray their interests. However loud and however numerous may be one's professions of patriotism, we all should know that he only is really patriotic who is trying to do for his country what he is conscious God meant his country to be!

With this definition, then, we begin — that patriotism is the love of the country's soul, the national idea, as expressed in a constant attempt to make the idea real. Do I say, "I love liberty, truth, justice, righteousness?" Then it is my duty to make liberty, truth, justice, righteousness actual facts, and not mere words. Do I say, "I love my country?" Then it is my duty so to live that all my acts shall conduce to my country's good; making a contribution of my best powers of mind and soul to my country's benefit. If power or place is given me, then I must use the advantages which this affords for laboring for my country's welfare. If I use them for my own self-aggrandizement and my own gain, I am no patriot, but a false and perjured man. If power and place do not come, and I continue in humble life, no less is it my duty to be the most of a man I am able to be, that so I may serve my country faithfully in whatever station God sees fit I should fill. I am to seek no office, I am to ask no favor of any government, I am to be no dependent upon the public treasury, I am simply to do my duty as a man, and give myself thus to my country's service. Otherwise I lose my independence, and being merely a slave to party, I put myself on a level with the beasts of whom the Hebrew prophet once spoke: "Verily, the ox knoweth his owner, and the ass his master's crib!"

There are one or two popular mistakes concerning patriotism, which it may be necessary to consider. One is, that patriotism consists in fealty to party. Party organizations are always transient. They are based upon some particular phase of public sentiment, and their end is success in a popular election for the purpose of gaining power. As a matter of course, partisan views are narrow. They embrace a very small portion of that which belongs to national greatness and the national good. As a consequence, they narrow the mind of him who adopts them, and belittle the character of his manhood. His thoughts pass in a narrow channel, and his soul is contracted in all its action. All his principles of morality are comprised in devotion to partisan objects. Even his religion is stained by his idolatry to the party gods, so that there can be no more deplorable sight than that of a man who sacrifices all his best and purest feelings at this unholy shrine, and, becoming infatuated by his long servitude, denies the principles upon which the life of his country rests, repudiates the sentiments for which the fathers fought and suffered, and at the voice of party dictation, makes truth and conscience and a righteous will nothing but empty names! When a political organization departs from the national idea, it is essentially unpatriotic, whatever its name and whatever its professions, and they who serve it to the neglect of other things, are no true patriots. A man must be independent of party trammels, and rebellious against party drill, and act out his own convictions, letting the party take care of itself. Parties shift with the changing circumstances of the times, and the prospects of victory; but the national idea remains the same, and he that would best serve his country must be faithful only to that!

2. Another mistake which men are liable to fall into is, that subservience to the existing government is patriotism. Good citizens must of course obey the laws, or if they find that the laws are contrary to conscience, they must be willing to suffer the consequences of disobedience; or if laws are so oppressive as not to be obeyed without the grossest injustice, and there can be no remedy except by resistance, they have the reserved right of revolution. In every nation there are

certain principles, established and sure, which are understood and agreed upon by all the people, or a majority of the people. But the government may be, and, in all countries, at some time, is opposed to and contrary to these principles. Written constitutions are the fundamental principles; if the government is opposed to these, then subservience to the government is not patriotism. It is patriotic then to oppose the government, that itself may be brought back to obedience to the Constitution, which is its master, as it is the people's master. This then is the use of the Constitution, to restrain the government from usurpation and protect the people in their rights; and sometimes, it may be, as it was in the case of Sir Thomas More, as it was in the case of Cromwell and his associates, as it was in the case of our Revolutionary Fathers, the highest duty of patriotism to oppose, to the very death, the existing government. If success come, the government is brought back to its allegiance; if defeat, the true patriot dies at his post, with his harness on.

3. Another mistaken idea of patriotism is that which connects it with an advocacy of all that is done within the boundaries of the country, whatever may be its character. Human nature is the same in all men, and in all countries many deeds are done which no true man can approve. Because there may be a foul wrong done by those who bear the same national name with one's own, and because it may have grown to an institution, and be recognized and supported by the law, it does

not follow that one must yield it his commendation, as a duty of patriotism. Nay, there may be a whole section of the country engaged in the sustentation of a social state, which the whole civilized world rebukes and denounces, and which all moral law and religious truth condemn, yet it by no means follows that an attempt to rid the country of such wrong is sectional and disorganizing. On the contrary, that is the best and purest patriotism which directs all the action of those who love truth and justice, and the interests of mankind to the overthrow of such an institution, that the national reproach may be removed, and the country no longer bear the censure of civilization, and the law of human progress. Shall we say that our country can do no wrong? It is foolish, as well as wicked, to claim to be immaculate, and refuse to be penitent. It is better, more manly and more brave, to acknowledge our faults and seek their remedy.

"Our country! right or wrong!
That were a traitor's song.
Let no true patriot's pen such words indite!
Who loves his native land,
Let him with heart, voice, hand,
Say, 'country or no country, speed the right!'

"Our country! right or wrong!
O, man of God! be strong!
Take God's whole armor for the holy fray.
Gird thee with truth! make right
Thy breast-plate; in the might
Of God, stand steadfast in the evil day!

"Our country! right or wrong!
Each image of the throng
Of ghastly woes, that rise upon thy sight;
O, let it move thy heart
Man! man! whoe'er thou art,
To say, 'God guide our struggling country right!'"

II. Accepting these propositions as true, our next inquiry is: How do they apply to us as American young men, and what are the duties that belong to us as patriots? Our first task, in this respect, is to ascertain, if possible, what is the American idea? what is the soul of our national life? Is there any particular design which Providence had in the production and continuance of our national life? In this matter it is especially necessary, situated as we are with respect to suffrage and its exercise, and the personal relation in which each one of us stands to the government which we sustain, and the power we organize for the support of our political state, that we should know what we ought to do. We ought to know it, too, beyond the possibility of mistake.

What then is the American idea? That is the main question. We must go to American history to find its answer. So far as we know what that history is, I am convinced that there was a great Providential design in the discovery and settlement of this country. Regard the time! Not till the old world had grown really old in civilization, not till true ideas of religion and government had become known in Europe, did the Western continent rise out of its long slumber beneath the waves. The latest to appear upon the stage of history, it did not appear before its time. Thousands of years passed away before the world was ready for the birth of America. This was the last and fairest child of time. All unknown it lay beyond the waste of waters, across whose bosom no adventurous navigator had passed, till Providence inspired Columbus with hope and longings for a land beyond the sea. I use the word inspired, for that idea which haunted his mind was an inspiration. It was something more than a love of adventure. It was something more than a desire for novelty, or even a love of fame. The various traditions which spoke of a land in the West, as they floated about the popular mind, might have led his thoughts in the direction of the truth. But others beside Columbus knew these traditions. God selected his agent with infinite wisdom, and led him by successive steps to the formation of the opinion that "there was undiscovered land in the western part of the ocean; that it was attainable; that it was fertile; and, finally, that it was inhabited." When he "had formed his theory," says his biographer, "it became fixed in his mind with singular firmness, and influenced his entire character and conduct. He never spoke in doubt or hesitation, but with as much certainty as if his eyes had beheld the promised land. No trial or disappointment could divert him from the steady pursuit of his object. A deep religious sentiment mingled with his meditations, and gave them, at times, a tinge of superstition, but it was of a sublime and lofty kind; he looked upon himself as standing in the hand of Heaven, chosen from among men for the accomplishment of its high purpose; he read, as he supposed, his contemplated discovery foretold in holy writ, and shadowed forth darkly in the mystic revelations of the prophets. The ends of the earth were to be brought together, and all nations, and tongues, and languages, united under the banners of the Redeemer." Such an idea as was this of Columbus sent him through Europe —

> "One faith against a whole earth's unbelief,
> One soul against the flesh of all mankind."

He laid his prospects before kings; he treated with them as an equal. Through many discouragements and many failures, sufficient to discourage a less hopeful man, he followed his purpose till he found a woman willing to listen to his proposal, and willing to risk her personal property upon the issue of the undertaking. He was successful, and his great success has made the name of Isabella of Castile a household word in all the homes of the New World. His great enterprise was at last consummated, and a new continent was given to humanity and civilization. Before his time, indeed, the shores of America had been reached by the brave sailors of Northern Europe. The green clad hills which overlook the waters of the beautiful Narraganset were trod by the foot of the Norsemen, nearly a thousand years ago; and so beautiful then were the islands and the surrounding coasts, and so fruitful in grapes and vines, that they were called Vinland. But the visits of these hardy navigators were of little consequence, and had no great results. Dissensions and strifes, even to bloodshed, destroyed their little colony, and the story of their wanderings, preserved in the sagas of Norway and Sweden, however interesting to us, has no large place in history. The time was not ripe for such a movement of the world's forces as was that of the voyages of Columbus. Yet even this was not the time, nor was the land which Columbus discovered the place, for the settlement of that portion of the continent which was to determine the character and destiny of the whole. The success of the heroic Genoese emboldened others to make a similar attempt and gain a like success, till gradually the whole coast line from Newfoundland to the Spanish Main, and around the Cape to Peru and the distant California, became known to European navigators. But it was not till democratic principles had become incorporated into the English constitution; it was not till the Protestant Reformation had been assured of triumph, that this country was settled, and then it was settled for the most part by Protestant Englishmen, and by those brave Hollanders who had learned, under the leadership of the great William of Orange, how to resist oppression, and by brave endurance to conquer the wrongs of despotism. Had it been settled at an earlier period, and by men of a different nation and religion, its whole subsequent history might have been changed. Compare the past history and the present condition of the Spanish American States with those of our own, and notice the difference. It is something more than the influence of climate, and something greater than the power of association. The difference is in the whole constitution and character of the different countries. Our superiority now is unquestioned, and if we do not lose it by our own sin and wrong, we shall have the greatest possession ever given a nation to enjoy. Believing in Providence, as we do, and recognizing an overruling wisdom in the direction of human events, there can be nothing clearer than the providential design in which our country had its birth. It was nothing less than this! If we have any skill in tracing the course of human life, we can not fail to see that God intended that on this soil, free from the prejudices of the ancient civilization, and safe from its errors, a nation should grow up to be the embodiment among the nations of the earth, of the democratic idea, which is a Christian idea, of liberty and self-government, civil and religious liberty, for all men within its borders. Whether we regard the physical features of the country, its varied climate, its unsurpassed fertility of soil, or the scarcity of its aboriginal inhabitants, the character of its first permanent settlers, or the conduct of those who planted the seeds of the Republic, the conclusion in any and all cases is inevitable, that here was the place, and this age of history the time, and this race the people, who were to inaugurate the successful supremacy of democratic ideas in national life. Here man, as such, living in all the power and dignity of his manhood beneath the open sky and over all this fair land, was to be greater than the State. The necessities of all manly culture were to mould the policy and direct the history of the nation. Sovereignty was to reside not in a titled nobility, or a pampered royalty, but in man; bearing the seal of liberty on his free forehead, and holding in his own strong hand the sceptre of a more than regal authority. Manhood against all king-craft, against all priest-craft, against all craft of whatever kind — this is the title of American nobility. If we sometimes forget it, and make ourselves appear foolish in our subservience to other and weaker things, it is to our shame and sorrow. The idea, the theory of our life is true, however we may falsify it in practice.

Let us see how the Fathers regarded it! In the depth of winter, in the year 1620, a little, shattered vessel lay at anchor, after a tempestuous voyage across the sea, in the harbor of Cape Cod. It was more than a century since Columbus had made known the existence of the new world. And if he then worked with a secret and uncomprehended consciousness of the Providential wisdom which had guided him, so did they also who made up the company of the Mayflower. They had, in their own language, "a great hope and inward zeal of laying some good foundation for the propagating and advancing the gospel of the kingdom of Christ in these remote parts of the world." That this hope might be realized, so far as civil government could make it real, the passengers of the Mayflower, before they stepped foot upon the shores of the world they had so long desired to see, assembled on the deck of the vessel as she lay within sight of the land, and by unanimous action, adopted the following simple compact: "In the name of God, amen. We, whose names are underwritten, having undertaken for the glory of God and advancement of the Christian faith and [the] honor of our king and country a voyage to plant the first colony in the northern parts of Virginia, do by these presents solemnly and mutually, in the presence of God and of one another, covenant and combine ourselves together into a civil body politic, for our better ordering and preservation, and furtherance of the ends aforesaid; and by virtue hereof, to enact, constitute and frame such just and equal laws, ordinances, acts, constitutions and offices, from time to time, as shall be thought most meet and convenient for the general good of the colony, unto which we promise all due submission and obedience." Each man signed this document. There were forty-one who appended their names, and these with their families constituted the first American democracy. They chose their governor, and thus began the colony of Plymouth. Bancroft does not hesitate to call this action "the birth of popular constitutional liberty." Another historian writes in glowing language: "This was the birth of Individual Liberty, of Democracy! and thus were organized the rights of man. Each man, master and servant, thenceforward was recognized as a man, felt the responsibility of a man, and voted as a man. The time had come, in the history of the world, when, in a civilized, organized community at Plymouth, on the Massachusetts shore, this recognition of individual liberty was to be a right — a right which neither seeks nor allows superior privileges to king, or priest, or aristocracy, but only the elevation and perfection of man whatever may be his condition or birth."

New-England was filled with the same sentiments, as its different parts were colonized. When Rhode-Island was established as a separate colony under Roger Williams, it ordained the following constitution: "We, whose names are here underwritten, being desirous to inhabit in the town of Providence, do promise to submit ourselves in active or passive obedience to all such orders, or agreements, as shall be made for the public good of the body, in an orderly way, by the major consent of the present inhabitants, masters of families, incorporated together into a township, and such others whom they shall admit unto the same — only in civil things." This was in 1638. And in 1641 an act was passed as follows: "It is ordered and unanimously agreed, that the government which this body politic doth attend unto in this Island is a Democracy." And Roger Williams declared in the "Bloody Tenet" that "the sovereign power of all civil authority is founded in the consent of the people." The other New-England colonies partook of the same spirit, and though New-Hampshire was settled for purposes of trade, and Connecticut was under the government of the church, yet the traders were democratic, and the church had no bishop. Indeed, had I time now to discuss the matter, I think I could show you that it was the grand old idea of Congregationalism in the churches, which knew no such thing as a hierarchy, either of Rome or England, that cultivated in the minds and character of the people of New-England that sturdy independence which has given our country all she has worth possessing. The people chose their own ministers as well as their own rulers, and in church and state still carried out to its results the principle of liberty. Even from the royal government in England, they demanded and received a recognition of the sovereignty of the people.

The democratic idea, though it was not realized in other parts of the country to so great an extent as in New-England, still found its expression, feeble though it might be in some quarters. It was difficult in a new land like this, to find a community which did not embody, in some degree, at least, the principle of individual freedom. The introduction of slaves into the Southern colonies hindered its course, as the institution of slavery now threatens its destruction. But the principle was then thought to be too strong to be greatly impeded. Let us hope that it now is too powerful to be subdued.

So, when the colonies combined into a nation in 1776, there was found through them all the same great purpose—to found an empire, which should express in permanent form, and declare before all mankind that there was one place, at least, on the face of the broad earth, where the individual man should be free, as God made him; that he should say who should be his ruler; and that all the power of him who was the governor should be derived only from the consent of those that were governed. Thus, the Declaration of Independence begins, after a short preamble, with the following statement: "We hold these truths to be self-evident, that all men are created equal; that they are endowed by their Creator with certain inalienable rights; that among these are life, liberty, and the pursuit of happiness; that to secure these rights, governments are instituted among men, deriving their just powers from the consent of the governed; that whenever any form of government becomes destructive of these ends, it is the right of the people to alter or abolish it and institute a new government." Familiar words are these, but they are the grand expression of grand ideas. Becoming the basis of national life, they become the grandest political statement ever uttered by human lips. Shall they be called, in the sneering language of a heated political discussion, by men who owe all they have to the freedom which they give, nothing but "sounding and glittering generalities;" nothing but "the passionate manifesto of a revolutionary struggle?" The facts of history contradict such faithless words, and the memory of the fathers should palsy forever the lips that are shameless enough to utter them! The men who made the Declaration of Independence, and the men who won independence, were not accustomed to deal in abstractions. They did nothing hastily or without deliberation; they were not carried away by excitement, nor hurried into acts of passion and resistance to fancied wrongs. They wrought in that deep sincerity which makes all work sublime, and conscious of the responsibility which they assumed, laid the foundations of a state in prayer and self-sacrifice, and nobleness, and honor, and truth; and placed as the very corner-stone the Christian idea of the worth of man, and the great principle of self-government. They sealed their declaration with their blood, and consecrated the American idea by the pains and triumphs of martyrdom. Shall we erect statues of brass and marble to their memory, and shall we be unfaithful to their principles?

When Independence was completely achieved, and the time came for establishing a true government, the representatives of the people formed a Constitution. Its opening words are these: "We, the people of these United States, in order to form a more perfect union, establish justice, insure domestic tranquillity, provide for the common defense, promote the general welfare, and secure the blessings of liberty to ourselves and our posterity forever, do ordain and establish this Constitution for the United States of America." Here, too, and in the provisions of the Constitution, the rights of the people were strictly guarded. Even the President himself is liable to impeachment by their representatives, if he violates his oath of office. And in the amendments to the Constitution occur the following remarkable words: "Congress shall make no law respecting an establishment of religion, or prohibiting the free exercise thereof; or abridging the freedom of speech, or of the press; or the right of the people peaceably to assemble and petition the government for the redress of grievances." The right of the people to bear arms was not to be infringed. Their houses and property were secured from unnecessary seizure and searchings, and they were never to have soldiers quartered upon them without their consent. Even in such minute particulars the right of the individual was jealously watched and protected. The whole spirit of American history breathes of liberty; liberty civil and religious, for all men within the borders of the American State! And that is the idea which claims to be, and is American. Only by that idea can the young man be governed in his political action.

I have been thus particular in stating what the American principle of government is, because it is especially necessary for the American young man to understand by what chart to shape his political course. If it be true that to us, in this day, are committed the destinies of civilization, we should be particular to have a clear and correct knowledge of our position, and what the interests of civilization demand of us. If we wish to be true patriots, if we wish to serve our country, we must be faithful to the principles on which our national life is based; the great principles of individual freedom, of civil and religious liberty under constitutional law, and the right of self-government. No young man going to his political duties can be justified in any course which does not distinctly and unequivocally recognize these principles, and fully carries them out to their practical application. He must not be deceived by names. He must not be governed by any prejudice. He must not be guided by personal ambition or the mean truckling to party, for the sake of emolument or office. The sacrifice of his manhood is too dear a price to pay for any party preferment, and no man can be in worse or more unmanly business than waiting upon Executive patronage. There is no greater curse to our young American manhood than this intense office-seeking, which runs like an epidemic through all classes of political life. There is so much which is lamentable in it, that I always feel more like condoling with a friend than congratulating him, if by any unfortunate chance he becomes an office-holder. In it there is very little patriotism. The truest patriots to-day are not those who are found in public station, but those men who, honest, industrious, honorable men of work, are faithfully attending to their own business, and are forming, from day to day, that truthful character which enters into the national life, and makes up a nation of real men. So the young man should think less of office, and more of himself. Shakspeare puts into the mouth of Cardinal Wolsey, at the time of his fall from power, the following words, addressed to one of his adherents:

> "Cromwell, I charge thee, fling away ambition;
> By that sin the angels fell; how can man, then,
> The image of his Maker, hope to win by it?
> * * * * Be just, and fear not;
> Let all the ends thou aim'st at be thy country's,
> Thy God's, and truth's! Then, if thou fall'st,
> Thou fall'st a blessed martyr!"

III. Having ascertained what the American idea is, the young man must attempt to realize it in every proper and honorable way. Through his agency, if possible, the idea must find its expression in American life. This is to be done in part by taking the position, and firmly holding it, of equal and exact justice to all within the boundaries of the country. Here, each man's thought and speech go to produce public opinion, of whose nature I have spoken in a former lecture. Here, too, in some States of the Union, each man, with certain limitations, has the privilege of voting. He has a voice in the government of the country, and his particular vote determines in part the character of that government. Here, then, is a direct responsibility resting upon each one for that character. If it is tyrannical, if it refuses to give equal justice, if it does not recognize the rights of the governed, if it fails to secure the blessings of liberty; if it endeavors in any way to establish injustice and wrong, then each one of us is responsible for such a course, in some measure; and each one of us must do all in his power, according to the means given him, to put an end to such a government, and establish one that will be faithful to the American idea, and make justice and liberty facts. An un-American and an unpatriotic government does not deserve to live on American soil. How shall it be made to die? There are two legitimate ways; by public opinion and vote. So each one of us is bound to make the most of himself, and be true to himself as a man. He must, spurning all party dictation, make up his own opinions, think his own thoughts, and express them in his own way. Where, as it is with us, the State exists for the individual, and not the individual for the State, the tendency is to individual independence; and that tendency is a good one. So, as an American, each one must be just to himself. You say, that is very easy. Is it? I apprehend you will find that it is a very difficult thing for a man to be just to himself. If you think it an easy matter, ask yourself "Who has the keeping of my conscience? How much of it has my business? What part is in my sect? What in my party? What portion of it is in this lodge-room, or that council-chamber, or that political caucus? How much of it do I subject to the control of my associates, that I may gain this office, or secure that position, or obtain the other advantage I am looking for?" No, it is not so easy a thing. There are many who prefer to put their conscience into others' keeping! So do not you! If you would be a true patriot and be just to your country, you must first be just to yourself. Then will you help in educating public opinion. For a just man always is powerful, and influences others; and if he thinks freely and acts freely, he is doing his part toward making freedom a national fact. His opinion, expressed with all the force that belongs to justice, will be like a mighty lever lifting up the weight of social and political truth that now lies helpless, and overthrowing the mass of social and political falsehood that threatens to crush his country's liberties!

2. We must, as American young men, always cherish a love of liberty, and in our political discussions keep prominently in view the great idea which underlies the American nationality. As a general rule, we shall be on the right side when we lean most to the side of liberty. When we begin to find ourselves sanctioning, even in the slightest manner, or under any pretext, what we know to be wrong and unjust, and opposed to freedom, we may begin to doubt the sincerity of our patriotism. We must examine ourselves; we must go back to the first principles of our national life, and find in them the test by which to judge of our-

selves and the measures of the national policy. How, for instance, is a public measure, recommended by government, and supported by a strong party, to be regarded? In the troubles of the period men seem scarcely to know what to do. The young man needs to have some way of judging. I apprehend that there is but one way. That way is to ascertain how far this measure is in accordance with the design and soul of the American nation, and how far it is at variance from it. It is not a question of party allegiance, or party success, or party defeat; not a question of personal profit to ourselves; not a question even of the country's peace and quiet. But it is a question of fidelity or unfaithfulness to the American idea. Does such a measure deny the truth of human equality in rights? Does it deny the democratic principle of self-government? Does it give to government any power not derived from the consent of the governed? Does it deny justice and freedom to any community in the land, and, opposed to their wishes, can only be forced upon them by the aid of military power? If these questions are to be answered in the affirmative, if human rights are infringed, if injustice is practiced, if government depends upon violence and force, then is such a measure, in all its features, un-American and unpatriotic. Nay, it is treasonable to every principle of the American State. It is a matter of very little consequence to us, who support or who oppose it; whether it has this or that great name upon its side or against it; whether it is affirmed or denied by this political caucus or party convention. We have something greater and more important than any man or body of men, the greatest name or the most ingeniously worded partisan platform. We have through all the history of the colonies, and the early days of the republic, the plainest declaration of the American idea. He that runs may read. It is by that that every political measure is to be judged. If in accordance with that, it must receive our approval; if opposed to that, it must receive our unqualified condemnation. Let us go to no man and to no platform short of the fundamental principles of our national life, to learn our political duties. Those principles are sufficient for us. Under their guidance let us do our political work, though we have to do it alone. Then we shall discharge our duty, and we must be willing to leave the consequences with God. He will take care that no just or righteous deed will fail or have an evil result.

3. Thus must the young man learn to apply his principles when the time comes for him to vote. In a country like ours, suffrage should be as free as is compatible with the safety of our institutions. Limitations in respect to color are essentially un-American. Limitations in respect to foreign birth, except such as provide for a residence sufficiently long to understand the nature of suffrage, the bearing of our political questions, and the character of our system of government,

are equally un-American. Limitations in respect to property belong to the same class; because our theory is, that a man is a man, rich or poor, and the fact of his manhood gives him the right to say who shall be his governor. Two thousand years ago Plato said, A city or state established upon property qualification "must necessarily lose its unity, and become two cities or states, one comprising the rich, and the other the poor; who reside together upon the same ground, and are always plotting against one another." I think it is as true now as then. Limitations in respect to education are, on the other hand, particularly necessary; for no one ought to deposit his ballot unless he can at least read the name which is on it, and understand the constitution which gives him the right to vote. I consider it one of the most solemn and prayerful duties which a man has to perform in our country — this of voting. He should vote, if he have the power, upon all occasions, even if he can find no one whom he may think more worthy to vote for than himself. I know there are some who make it a matter of conscience to abstain from voting altogether — the much maligned and calumniated Abolitionists. But though I think them mistaken in this matter, I can not but respect the honesty of their opinions, and the ability and self-devotion with which they maintain them. But there are thousands among us who have no scruple upon the subject, but who are utterly careless and indifferent about the matter. I think they are neglecting what is to me a most imperative duty — nay, a religious duty, for the performance of which a man is held responsible before God. Of course, it does not belong to me to say with what particular party a man should vote, except that he should vote, if he would be really patriotic, with that organization which most of all embodies the principles of liberty and justice. Vote somehow a man must, and if he can find no party which does embody the American idea, then let him stand, if he can stand no where else, in a bare minority of one. There is an advantage, sometimes, in standing alone. One is generally sure of being in the company of an honest man. He is also safe from the temptation of his integrity, involved in an election to public office. Never allow yourself, young man, to be relied upon as a party man, but vote, when the time comes, not according to your neighbor's opinions, but your own true conviction! Other such men may readily be found, and as ten righteous men acting boldly and truly could have saved Sodom, so might there arise a combination of men founded on the real American idea of liberty for all men in the country, and liberty for all mankind.

IV. The fourth great duty of patriotism is to oppose all powers which array themselves against the American idea. Now the most insidious and the most powerful foe with which we have to deal, comes in the guise of republicanism, and bears on its lips the sacred name of liberty! The Roman church makes no pretensions to republicanism, and is an anomaly among us; which I believe, in a fair field and an open contest can not stand. I think our fears respecting it are much exaggerated. But there is a foe, which, in its unscrupulous disregard of all the rules of honorable warfare; in its determined hostility to every principle of liberty; in its alliance with ignorance, and injustice, and falsehood, plots the overthrow of all free institutions and the national fabric itself. There is a foe which is most of all to be dreaded, and most of all to be fought against — the institution of slavery. Never was any thing more false, more arrogant, more faithless, more aggressive, more despotic than this power. In the name of democracy it builds up the most aristocratic oligarchy. In the name of liberty it threatens treasonably to overthrow the Union. It breaks its treaties in the name of faith. It tramples upon the Declaration of Independence in the name of the Constitution. It cowardly crushes the weak in the name of chivalry. It impiously oppresses and traffics in the image of the Father in the name of religion and of God! Here is the great enemy to the American idea. It gives us battle every moment that we live; it seizes upon free territory, that it may perpetuate its existence; it would legalize piracy that it may extend its dominion. By the falsification of history and the distortion of law, it would make every place over which the American flag floats, the soil of slaves. The President, from his high position, has recently declared, that, by the recent decision of the Supreme Court, "Kansas," (and the principle applies to all the Territories of the nation) "is as much a slave State as Georgia or South-Carolina." Is it necessary that I should trace its progress from the times when such men as Washington, Franklin, Henry, George Mason, the Adamses, and Jefferson, opposed it, until now, when it makes the atrocious statement which I have just quoted? Need I say how it has triumphed in all the great contests since the formation of the Constitution? In fixing the ratio of representation; in deferring the abolition of the slave trade for twenty years; in compelling the rendition of fugitive slaves; in spurning Franklin with his anti-slavery petition from the bar of Congress; in purchasing Louisiana; in the admission of Missouri; in the annexation of Texas; in the legislation of 1850; in the repeal of the Missouri Compromise in 1854; in all these it has succeeded. When has it not succeeded? By the aid of venal and traitorous men, it has always carried out its plans of aggression, and now it stands more lustful of power and more arrogant than ever before. With one hand it throttles the Supreme Court, with the other it crushes the President and his Cabinet. It presses with its heavy foot upon the legislative departments; it points the cannon of army and navy; it breaks open the Post-Office; it plunders the Treasury; it reads history falsely; it outrages the law. What it can not accomplish by bribery, it does by force. When it can not vote by ballot, it sends its hordes of ruffians to take possession of the polls; when it can not legislate by free discussion and positive majorities, it uses the bludgeon and the bowie-knife; when it fails to gain the victory, it makes the triumph of freedom barren of results. Every where is its influence felt. There is no amenity of social intercourse which it does not rudely destroy; there is no tie of domestic life which it does not sever. There is no principle of morality, civilization and religion which it does not violate. It has made labor disgraceful; it has created that prejudice which has disfranchised the black man in a majority of the nominally free States; which refuses him equal rights in education, and denies his manhood. It degrades the national character; it poisons the national life; it weakens the national influence. It degrades our own manhood through all our days. Beginning with the enslavement of black men, it seeks now to reduce white men to abject submission. Beginning with an unjust representation, it now aims at destroying the principle of self-government altogether!

I speak on this subject, not as a politician, not as a partisan, but as a man, who desires to know what his duty is in a crisis like the present; as a man, too, who is accustomed to look at these and all other matters from the stand point of Christian principle, and to bring all things to the test of what I know to be right and true; and, speaking so, I can not but think that in the struggle now in progress the interests of all our civilization are involved. It is not partisan defeat which is threatened, but national death; and national death would be the knell of millions in both hemispheres of the globe. God meant that this American state should be the herald to all the world of a kingdom of righteousness, freedom and peace; on whose soil should be grown the loftiest manhood; whose atmosphere should be electric with the grandest ideas; whose influence, as a nation, should be felt to the remotest corner of the globe for the good of all mankind. Shall we attempt to thwart this design? Shall we be false to the sublime ideal of a state which was in the Fathers' mind? Let us awake from our dream of sloth and ease, and prove ourselves worthy of the history that ennobles us. Slavery is plotting our destruction! Slavery is making us a disgrace before the world! Shall we suffer it, my brothers? No! a thousand times no! In the name of a Christian patriotism let us be faithful to our national idea and our national life!

Here, then, to sum up, are the duties of patriotism: To understand the idea of our national existence — to love that idea of justice and liberty with our whole soul — to devote ourselves to its fulfillment with all our might, and to oppose whatever may militate against its progress. These duties come to us as American young men, and appeal to us with overwhelming force. It is not to be questioned that the young men of America are the hope of the nation.

Within the next quarter century, nay, within the present decade of years, the question is to be determined whether liberty or oppression is to bear rule for all the future. It is for us to determine whether this grand experiment of republicanism shall result in success or failure; whether despotism or freedom shall triumph on these western fields.

The conflict hastens on. I look out into the future, not with despondency but with hope. If we are faithful, the issue is not doubtful. The interests of civilization are on our side. God's providence can not fail. Not a word spoken, not a deed done in behalf of liberty and justice, can be lost. From all the places of human life, where manly resolution, where faithful adherence to principle, where self-devotion, courage, patriotism, have left the impress of their nobleness upon human life, and made the scene of their manifestation glorious, come voices of encouragement and hope. Let us not falter; let us not be desponding. Our country demands our patient, persevering, steady, cheerful action for liberty, for humanity, for God! We may not witness the entire redemption of our land, but the time will come when the American idea will be realized, and a genuine republicanism make all men free within the nation's boundaries! Other men will enter into our labors, and in due time the fields will be white for the harvest!

"We can not falter! Did we so,
The stones beneath would murmur out,

And all the winds that round us blow
  Would whisper of our shame about.
No ! let the tempest rock the land !
Our faith shall live ! our truth shall stand !

" True as the Vaudois hemmed around
  With Papal fire and Roman steel,
True as the Christian heroine bound
  Upon Domitian's torturing wheel,
We bate no breath ! we curb no thought !
COME WHAT MAY COME ! WE FALTER NOT !"

VII. THE YOUNG MAN IN THE CHURCH.

In concluding this series of addresses, I feel that I can select no better subject than that which supports, and embraces, and crowns a manly character, namely, a true religion. Our course would be as incomplete without the consideration of this subject, as a young man's character would be incomplete without the presence of religious principle. As in the arch, which the builder raises, there is necessary the keystone to make his work firm and durable; so in the structure which we have here, through the last three months, been endeavoring to plan, we need the keystone of religion to complete our labors and make the edifice strong.

In treating our present subject,—the Young Man in the Church,—that I may show you what should be the character of a young man's religion, I shall speak of the nature and form of religion itself; the universality of its application; the manliness of a religious character, and its influence upon life. I think I shall be able to show you that our subject is the most practical we have yet considered.

Before we enter directly upon the discussion, however, it seems necessary to make a few preliminary remarks, that I may meet the objections which young men sometimes have to a consideration of a subject like this. There are ideas which to me appear erroneous, but which still have their place in a young man's mind. If we can succeed in dispossessing them, we shall do a great service, not only to ourselves but to all with whom we have intercourse.

1. It is often the case that we are inclined to look upon religion as something we do not need in early life. Our days now pass on without much that embitters them, and, regarding religion rather as a retreat from care, or a consolation from sorrow, or a refuge from the ills of life, than as an active principle, which is the inspiration of all life, we leave, to the convenient season of mature age, the consideration of a subject which is suited for graver years. Now, we think religion would interfere with the pleasures of our youth; it would cast a shadow over the brightness of these happy days; it would make us sombre and serious, when our hearts should be filled with a more natural joy; and we should become old before our time. We entirely mistake the character of religion when thus we suppose it is for our safety only that we must become religious; that, because we need solace, and support, and rest, when we are sad, and weak, and weary, we should fly to the strengthening influences of religion; that because there are evil days in the prospect, we should provide some shelter from the fury of the tempest which they will bring with them. We en-

tirely mistake the character of religion when we suppose it is to diminish our pleasures, or make us too grave, or darken our days, or produce premature old age. It is a mistake to suppose that religion is nothing more than a convenient refuge for a man when he has become sick and tired of the world, and has found an earthly life empty and unsatisfactory; that it is an expedient for his salvation from the threatened woes of the future, which his conscience dreads. No, I shall advocate religion as a principle, to make us more manful, more dutiful, more true; as suited particularly to the season of youth; as an experience of the soul, which will enhance the enjoyment of life; which will make the daily toil easier and more blessed; which, instead of making the life sad, will fill it with happiness; and, instead of producing untimely age, will keep the heart fresh and young through all the days of a man's life, and never allow it to grow old! Religion is the power of a man's soul in the present life, and far more concerns itself with the duties of the present hour than with a way of escape from the merited punishment of one's wrong-doing in the future. It belongs to the life of to-day, and the scenes of time, as well as, and possibly even more than, to the life of to-morrow and the scenes of eternity.

2. Another mistake which people fall into, and which in its practical consequences produces a distaste to religion in the young man's mind, is the habit with some religious people of regarding religion as something to

be obtained, rather than cultivated and grown. Many persons say "get religion" very much in the same way, and with the same manner, as a worldly man would advise his son, "Get money—honestly if you can, but by all means get money." So religion is to be obtained by subjecting one's self to certain religious influences, which thus become a kind of religious machinery, and the product of which is mechanical and formal. Young men are accustomed to look at matters in a common-sense and natural way. They do not believe in formalism. They rebel against authority. It is a natural state of the mind, and can not be prevented, and if religion is presented in a formal and mechanical way, it becomes offensive to them. And the result is, they absent themselves from the presence of religious influences of all kinds, and soon cease to obey religious sanctions. They begin to doubt religious truths, and soon fall into that supercilious and irreligious frame of mind which sneers at and derides all moral and religious declarations; and if they do not fall into utter atheism, they find themselves in that condition which believes nothing and hopes for nothing!

3. Another mistake which in its results repels young men from religion, is to suppose that all the deeds that are done in the name of religion are the results of religious workings. As the young man reads history, he can not fail to find the story of persecution, of intolerance, of bigotry. His moral sense tells him that

these are wrong. He is willing and even glad to witness the triumphs of Christianity, as it has made its way along through the ages. But he is interrupted in his joy by the tales of cruelty that stain the pages of the Church's life. He sees the wrong that has been done to man in the name of God. He finds that they, who were to be known as disciples of Christ by the love which they were to have one toward another, are filled with hatred, and variance, and strife. As he hears the clank of fetters, and sees the smoke that rises from the stake whereon men have suffered for conscience' sake, and beholds the sword of the executioner dripping with the blood of martyrdom; and as he remembers that the crimes at which humanity shudders have been committed by men calling themselves Christian, he has lost their faith in religion altogether, and has felt that it is all a falsehood. If these are its legitimate fruits, he does not wish to be known as its adherent. If, too, the meanness, the cant, the hypocrisy, and Phariseeism, which the Church too often shelters, are to be taken as products of the life of the Church, he wishes for nothing of the kind. It is a fact that is too conspicuous, and which does more to make religion distasteful to young men than almost any other influence in our time, that most men, sensible, practical, shrewd in all other relations and actions, when they come to speak of religion and its duties, seem to lose their good sense, their practical wit and shrewdness, and utter themselves in solemn commonplaces, and unmeaning and inexpressive religious phrases. Talk of business, and they surprise you with their plain and practical good sense, and their knowledge of human nature. Talk of politics, and they are full of all wise suggestions. But talk of religion, and they are either dumb, or they have a flow of sounding words whose significance or aptness it is utterly impossible to perceive. They either say nothing, or have such a lingual power that it overwhelms you. Like Talkative, in Pilgrim's Progress, they "talk of things heavenly or things earthly; things moral or things evangelical; things sacred or things profane; things past or things to come; things more essential or things circumstantial." But what Christian said of Talkative, that "all he had lay in his tongue, and his religion was to make a noise therewith," is also true of these men who have, if not an immortality, at least an eternity of speech. There may be much in the character of professed religious men to disgust the generous and earnest youth, who naturally looks for consistency between profession and practice, between speech and action. He may find meanness, and narrowness, and selfishness, and dishonesty, where he expected to witness the opposite qualities of character, and, in his haste, he may condemn religion. But he does not remember that these are not the true products of a religious character. If they appear, it only shows that the man who exhibits them is really deficient in religious principles, and has yet to learn what religion is. Let the man be censured for his falseness, but let not religion be held responsible for such practices. It is not because he is a religious man that he engages in them, but because he is devoid of religion.

I. Our first inquiry then must be into the nature of religion itself. Religion signifies the union of man with God. I believe it to be a natural condition and state of the soul. It is because man is a child of God; the creature of his power; the ward of his guardianship; the recipient of his love; that he is essentially a religious being. Religion belongs to the best part of man's nature; and, thus belonging to him, he becomes most of a man when he is most truly and most thoroughly religious. I need not now attempt to show how universal is the existence of the religious sentiment. It is found wherever man lives, and, though in some instances it may be existing in the midst of ignorance, barbarism and degradation, it is still in the soul of man. He builds temples to his gods; he erects shrines and altars where he may offer up his worship; he gives to his deity the dearest possessions of his life; he immolates himself, if conscious that an offended god requires the sacrifice. We can not find a tribe of people so degraded as to be without religion of some kind. They must worship something, if it be but the elemental familiar phenomena which appear in their daily life. There has been no age of history which has not borne witness to the existence of this power of religion. Indeed, we can not read history aright, even of heathenism itself, unless we take into the account the religious element of human nature, and its influence upon human life. Through all the past we find men facing the great questions which demand their answer in the discussions of to-day. They bow before the sense of the supernatural. They inquisitively search for the origin of their existence. They attempt to investigate the nature of their souls. They strive to pierce the clouds that hang over the grave, and ascertain the mysteries of the future life. And though the endeavors to settle these momentous questions may have been accompanied by deeds of dark and even terrible wrong, yet no man, who has traced the operations of the laws that govern his life, can fail to see that the noblest achievements of the human race in wisdom and love have been the result of the mental and spiritual activity which these endeavors have required! We can not interrogate any past age without receiving for answer the assurance that man has lived in obedience to divine laws; that he has recognized his dependence upon divine existences, and that all his hopes for what is best and fairest in life have been inspired by his consciousness of divine connections. How true is that word of St. Paul: "God hath made of one blood all nations of men, for to dwell on all the face of the earth, and hath determined the times before appointed, and the bounds of their habitation; that they should seek the Lord, if haply they might feel after him and find him, though he be not far from any one of us." The culture and learning of the Apostle had opened to him the fact, which had a profound philosophy in it, that God was present in the affairs of men; that his providence guided the nations in their course, and that their best endeavors in all intellectual and spiritual things were called forth in the search for the knowledge of "the unknown God." Yes, it is God that ruleth among the inhabitants of the earth as well as in the armies of Heaven. Nations, empires, whole races and tribes of men, live and die, and pass away into almost utter oblivion, but they do not pass without leaving the witnesses of their subjection to the control of their religious ideas, and of their devotion to the Being who determined their life. Call it superstition, if you will; but it is of a really sublime character, and it is deeply significant of the power of divine influence. Yes, it is God who orders all human life. No nation lives without his care and fatherly superintendence. In studying history we should never forget this great truth, but should strive to find those manifestations of a universal providence, which make history a revelation of God himself, recognizing in the thoughts and acts of men the "vestiges of him whose path is in the deep of time." Thus reverently would we tread the ways of life, and read the truth of the eternal God in the perishable works of man. The Eastern poet sings in lofty strains the divine perfections:

"There's a Godhead in attendance,
Unobserved by ear or eye;

There is a divine resplendence
On the darkness of the sky;
Highest of all heights o'ershading
In unmoved complacency;
Deepest of all depths pervading
In serene felicity.

"Sitting still, through space he travels;
Calmly resting, fills all time;
And to the pure heart unravels
E'en his attributes sublime.
Who desires him shall obtain him,
He who loves him, wins his love,
Till God's truth shall teach and train him
For the highest seats above."

Religion, however, in my view is somewhat more than a sentiment, residing within the spiritual nature of man, and then becoming the inspiration of worship. It does not occupy itself wholly in devotional aspiration. It belongs to all intellectual activity, and is the soul of all true philosophy. As a system of belief, as the incitement of the reason, as the strength of the intellect, and the power of all the best mental exertion of man, it extends beyond the domain of sentiment, and connects itself with the solution of all the problems with which the mind grapples. The most lasting of intellectual accomplishments are those which religion has been the means of effecting. I do not say, indeed, that the ablest men, intellectually speaking, have been the most religious men; but I think it is true, that there is no real and true ability in intellectual labor, which has not connections with the culture of the religious faculties. Intellectual truth must have a sure alliance with spiritual truth; and the man who works in the service of truth, of whatever kind, is working in the service of God, who is the source of truth. "The love of truth," embodying itself in all intellectual achievement, "is the natural and instinctive piety of the mind," says a recent writer. "In studying the facts of nature, material or human, I am studying the thought of God; for in the world of real things a fact is the direct speech of the Father. Words make up the language of men; facts and ideas are the words of God; his universal language to his children, in which he speaks from all eternity to all time. Man, "made in the image of God," loves his Father's thoughts, and is not contented till he hears that speech; then he is satisfied." This seems to me the proper work of the mental faculties; but it must be pursued with that expectant and hopeful energy which looks for more light constantly to break forth upon the truth of God. If the mind makes up its own system of religion, and declares that the theories which it may form respecting divine things are the truth, and there can be no progress beyond them; if it assumes to define what is not definable; if it sets up a creed or formula of religious truth, and declares that that establishes the bounds beyond which it is unsafe and dangerous to travel; thus putting its feeble speech against the word of the Almighty, it is evident that it is doing a work which is not legitimate. It transgresses its powers and deserves rebuke. It is impossible that the whole of divine truth is to be measured and guaged as one would measure a field or sound the depths of the sea. There may flow, indeed there does flow into each honest mind, some knowledge of divine realities, which the mind may be unable to repress; and there is no creed, however laboriously the intellect may have wrought in its formation, which can truly give form to the formless truth. Well does Prof. Park say: "In unnumbered cases the real faith of Christians has been purer than their written statements of it. Men, women and children have often decided when doctors disagreed; and doctors, themselves, have often felt aright when they have reasoned amiss. * * * * Where the school-room has transplanted the metaphors of the Bible to the rude exposure of logic, they are frozen up, their fragrance is gone, their juices evaporated, and their withered leaves are preserved as specimens of that which in its rightful place surpassed the glory of the wisest sage." If the Church so mistakes its mission to the world as to say that its peculiar system of doctrine teaches all that can be taught respecting religion; that it is profane to investigate farther and deeper, and that every thing beyond its pale is heresy and falsehood, the Church will suffer more than mankind. For men must think, as a matter of necessity; they must go beyond Church limits, and they will prefer a free and progressive heresy to a narrow and stationary orthodoxy. The mind feels that there are truths outside the creeds of the churches, and if the churches attempt to prevent investigation, they will find themselves suddenly powerless; for the reason, active in other things, will refuse to be inert in this. We may well believe that God gave men the powers of the reason, that they might be employed. If we do not employ them, we should be doing injustice to ourselves and an impiety toward him. Their highest use must be in the search for God's truth. That truth is greater than the Church, and if the Church stand in the way of its progress, it will be ground to powder, as Judaism was by Christianity; as Romanism will be by Protestantism; as Protestantism itself must be if it attempt to control the human mind, and is false to the great principle of its life — the right of private judgment. If the Church would exercise its power rightly upon human life, it must not assume to be the dictator to the mind, supreme and absolute, speaking by authority. It must rather be the teacher; ready itself to be taught, and willing to acknowledge that both teacher and disciples are but learners at the feet of Christ.

Religion has a wider function still. It concerns itself with the moral conduct of man, and thus becomes a practicable principle in the life. Its seat may be in the heart; it moves the brain to right and true thought; it directs the will that controls the practical work of human existence. It speaks from the tongue, in every true and sincere, every loving and generous word. It springs from the hand, in every faithful, earnest, and disinterested action. It works through all the toil of life, and leaves its blessing wherever its presence makes its way; so that it becomes the soul of all daily practice, as it is the spirit of the secret closet prayer. We misapprehend religion when we consider it merely as a sentiment, whose influence brightens the heart with a glow of devotional feeling, and induces an ecstatic state of soul, in which visions of heaven are enjoyed, or hushes it into the repose, which belongs to the indulgence of devout meditation. The devotee and the monk, isolated from the world, may find a pleasure in the seclusion of pious emotion, and may enjoy the luxury of prayer; but they lose half the faculty of life in their deprivation from the privilege of duty. Religion may become mysticism, as in the olden time it sent its disciples out into the desert, employing them upon useless labors, and separating them from association with their fellows; or, as at the present day, it pronounces all natural affection profane and wicked; separating its sanctions from the social and domestic life of man. We equally misapprehend religion, when we consider it as embodied in a creed, demanding assent, on pain of excommunication, and even refusing the opportunity of salvation except upon conditions of belief which the reason can not possibly accept. We equally misapprehend religion when we consider it as simply a system of works, and wholly residing in outward human conduct; when we harden it into a cold, stiff system of morality. We certainly misapprehend it when we attempt to separate it from our common daily life; when we shut it up in the church, and make it a Sunday observance and an ecclesiastical form. Religion belongs to the week-day life as well as the Sunday life; to the world of duty as well as the seclusion of piety; and there is not a word nor a deed of which it may not be the great informing spirit, unseen, yet present still!

Religion is not prayer, it is not belief, it is not duty. It is a combination of all these; a union of all the faculties of human nature, moving the entire man to all worthy and righteous life. It is the interior secret spirit, which works through all inward and all outward things; which fills all life; which moves the heart with all gentle and pure emotions; which guides the intellect into all right and correct thought; which shines through every deed, making the humblest act glorious, and dignifies every common duty, making the meanest office noble. It is the most vigorous faculty of man. It is the loveliest grace of woman. It beautifies the innocence of childhood. It consecrates the generous ambition of youth. It softens the formalities of middle age, and saving it from the canker of worldliness, makes it useful to the grandest results. It cheers the declining steps of age, dispelling the clouds that hang around the grave, and opening upon the darkness of the closing day of life the golden splendors of immortality. It separates us from no duty of the earth, but it fills that duty with the glory of heaven. It takes us away from no connection with time, but it fills it with all the power of eternity. It teaches while it inspires. It strengthens while it teaches; and in inspiration, instruction and action, it is the soul of all true life! It lights up the blackened walls of poor men's homes. It gilds anew the magnificence of rich men's mansions. The earth, the air, the sky, is all full of its glory! It applies every where. Its power is felt every where. It is present every where.

II. Religion having this nature, power and universality of application, we come next to consider its effect upon human character. We are sometimes inclined to think that a religious character has some portion of weakness and effeminacy. We say that it is unmanly to be occupied in religious service. It is soft and yielding. It resents no injury. It is meek and forgiving. It has not that brave and firm consistency of purpose, and resolution of action, which go through all dangers and difficulties, and meet death in its most terrible form without shuddering. We could not fall into a graver error. I affirm that a religious character is the manliest, the bravest, the firmest, the most heroic. There is no man so true and courageous as the genuinely religious man. Instead of shrinking from danger, he meets it with the boldest face and the most unflinching fortitude. Instead of retreating from difficulty, he fronts it with intrepid brow; he conquers it with the most resolute valor. Instead of avoiding death through fear, he does not hesitate to meet it, if it comes in the path of duty, without the blanching of a cheek or the quiver of an eye-lid. Cool, calm, collected, fearless, firmly standing to the right through disaster, defeat, torture, pain, and all things horrible, the truly religious man never falters or faints. If duty says, die in behalf of truth, he willingly lays down his life a sacrifice of all things dear to his right conviction! If in all ages he has been the noble and brave, who is willing to die for his country, how much nobler and braver must he be thought who is willing to die for humanity and God! who, widening the hope of his vision beyond the limits of his own home and country, sees himself bound to all mankind by the common tie of a common brotherhood, and goes to the frightfullest death, that they, who have no claim upon him but this common tie, may receive an eternal benefit! There is the highest kind of manliness, I think, in that.

There is manliness, too, in the meekness and the forgiving spirit which belong to the Christian character. Self-control is certainly a manly quality. To hold one's self in complete check; to have entire mastery over the passions; to be able to look calmly upon the wreck of all things that are choicely valued, and have no feeling of anger toward the man who caused it; nay, to forgive, when forgiveness is the most difficult thing to be done; these are not tokens of a weak but of a strong character. They do not indicate a timid, fearful, or unmanly man; but rather a man whose nobility of soul rises above the weakness of passion, and governs all the movements of his life with the force of religious principle. The Hebrew moralist understood the strength which resides in the constancy of dutiful self-control, when he said: "He that is slow to anger is better than the mighty; and he that ruleth his spirit, than he that taketh a city." There is no man that has held himself back, in moments of excited passion, but knows how much real bravery and firmness are required to keep the control of his spirit.

Certainly, there is manliness in a calm, and, as is often necessary, a solitary adherence to the truth through all vicissitudes of life. Then the lonely constancy to principle becomes heroic. I acknowledge, and am glad to appreciate the bravery, with which men enter into the conflict with terrible death upon the field of battle. But this, great as it may be sometimes, does not compare with the bravery which dares to stand alone and confront death — nay, confront life — for the sake of one's misunderstood and misapprehended truth. Confront life, I say, for it sometimes is easier to die than live. Nay, it is more brave and manly to live through and conquer misfortune than it is to yield one's life, and sink despondingly before it. It is comparatively easy, too, to stand fast in battle array, surrounded by numbers, and strengthened by the sympathy of companions. But it is not so easy to stand alone, with only truth and God, and defy a whole world of unbelief.

"Count we o'er earth's chosen heroes — they were men that stood alone,
While the men they agonized for, hurled the contumelious stone;
Stood serene, and, down the future, saw the golden beam incline
To the side of perfect justice, mastered by their faith divine,
By one man's plain truth to manhood, and to God's supreme design."

Well and bravely does an English preacher say: "In human things, the strength that is in a man can only be learned when he is thrown upon his own resources, and left alone. What a man can do in conjunction with others, does not test the man. Tell us what he can do alone. It is one thing to defend the truth when you know that your audience are already prepossessed, and that every argument will meet a willing response; and it is another thing to hold the truth when truth is to be supported, if at all, alone — met by cold looks and unsympathizing suspicion. It is one thing to rush on to danger with the shouts and sympathy of numbers; it is another thing when the lonely chieftain of the sinking ship sees the last boatful disengage itself, and folds his arms to go down into the majesty of darkness, crushed, but not subdued."

It must be the manliest of all things to be incited to all noble action by the consciousness of God's presence with us in the scenes of life, and the assurance of God's help in every dutiful work. To feel through all the various scenes and toils of life, that God's arm is the strength of ours; that his protecting care is always over us, and that we are laboring with him by every daily faithfulness. Certainly there is a dignity given to the commonest life thus, which redeems it from its commonness; which raises it from its obscurity, and which sets it on high in light. Listen to David: "He that dwelleth in the secret place of the Most High, shall abide under the shadow of the Almighty. Because thou hast made the Lord, who is my refuge, even the Most High, thy habitation, there shall no evil befall thee; neither shall any plague come near thy dwelling. I will set him on high, because he hath known my name. He shall call upon me, and I will answer him. I will be with him in trouble; I will deliver him and honor him." Hear Isaiah: "The Lord giveth power to the faint; and to them that have no might, he increaseth strength. Even the youths shall faint and be weary, and the young men shall utterly fail. But they that wait upon the Lord shall know their strength; they shall mount up with wings as eagles; they shall run and not be weary; they shall walk and not faint." And Jesus declares: "If a man love me, he will keep my words; and my Father will love him, and we will come unto him, and make our abode with him." And Paul expresses the same thought in his words to the Corinthians. "We are laborers together with God. Know ye not that ye are the temple of God, and that the spirit of God dwelleth in you?" It seems to me that

that is the manliest of all conditions in life, which thus possesses, as the grand power of all existence and all action, this indwelling presence, and this protecting care of the omniscient and omnipotent God; the all merciful and all loving Father!

If the young man desires to know of personal examples, he can find them wherever a true religion has become the motive power of a man's soul. First, I mention, in our own times, one of the most religious of men and one of the most manly of men, THOMAS ARNOLD. Placed in that most trying situation, the master of an English school, with the wills of an hundred boys to train into conformity with his own, and inspire them with his own noble purposes, and yet not to allow them to know till after years had revealed the course of discipline, how careful, how diligent, how observant of their interests, how judicious in his treatment he had always been, not forgetting the smallest, and impartial in his guidance of all; a broad, catholic, genial, liberal, cultivated man, without austerity, without hypocrisy, without pretense, without a particle of cant—his character adorns the annals of the Church as one of its most saintly and one of its most heroic men. Valorous, truthful and brave, he made an impression upon the English religious mind, such as no other man engaged in the great religious movements in England ever could have done. For it was not within the boundaries of a school-room that his influence was exerted, but through his pupils upon all England, and through England upon all Christendom; and not alone by means of his pupils, but by means of his manly and Christian writings. "The pupils," says one of his eulogists, "saw that their teacher was a true man and a Christian; the grasp of his energy they felt upon them; they knew not how, but the very air seemed pervaded by his influence. Accustomed to be treated as Christian gentlemen whose word was not to be called in question, they learned to shrink from meanness, to acquire self-command, and to make intelligence and nobleness their aims. At the university, youths from other quarters might excel in the quickness, the cleverness, and, it might even at times happen, the minute accuracy of school-boys; those from Rugby had the character, the thought, the deliberate purpose of men."

I have selected this instance out of many, because it is thought that boys are not susceptible to religious impressions, and that the period of youth is not favorable to religious growth. I believe that the fault is not in the nature of boys and young men, so much as it is in the character of the man who attempts to guide them in the way of religious truth. They are quick observers; they are keen in their judgment of character; if there is any thing like falsehood or cowardice, or a venal time-serving, they are sure to detect it, and when they lose their feeling of respect toward the man who teaches, there is an end of his influence. But if he is manly, true, without assumption and without forwardness, he will be always sure of attentive consideration, and his influence will always be felt for their good. An untrue and cowardly man is no fit teacher for boys, and they very soon know it. Thus a boys' school becomes a test of character, and he that faithfully abides it shows himself a just and manly man.

To go back a few years more remote, we come into the stormy times of the Reformation of the sixteenth century, and among those brave men who controlled the destinies of modern civilization, we find numerous instances of the power which religion gives for the performance of the manliest deeds. The bravest men of that period were men who were swayed by a religious purpose of doing God's will. Whether that purpose led them to the battle-field to strive for liberty of conscience and the salvation of the State; or to the pulpit and the public hall, to speak the words which were to move the nations to the way of truth; or to the stake and the dungeons of the Inquisition, to seal their testimony with their heart's blood, in every and in all cases they amply proved that the religion which they professed and practiced was far from making them unmanly; nay, it moved them, as with the strength of the Omnipotent. I need not mention to you such men as Wyclyf, as John Huss, as Ulric Zwingle, as Socinus, Luther, and Melancthon, as John Knox, Hampden, Robinson, and their brave associates; you know them as the world's heroes; you know them also as the world's religious men. What a grand word that was which William of Orange once said, showing that he too belonged to this glorious company! The Spanish tyrant, Philip II., had set the price of 25,000 florins of gold upon his head; for William was the main opponent to the scheme of the infatuated monarch, to force the Inquisition upon the people of Holland against their will. In the decree which the despot made — almost unparalleled in baseness — beside the offer of the money, there was also added the promise of nobility. If the murderer "have committed crime," says the royal command, "we will pardon him, and if he be not already noble, we will ennoble him." In the defiance which William hurled back, occur the following noble words: "I am in the hand of God; my worldly goods and my life have long since been devoted to his service. He will dispose of them as seems best for his glory and my salvation."

The annals of religious history are full of such records of bravery. In the early ages of the Church what instances of fearless martyrdom! The feeblest maiden seemed gifted with a more than manly courage, when the truth of Christ became the inspiration of her heart. She stood naked and defenseless in the arena of the Roman Amphitheatre without the movement of a muscle; calm as though she were on her knees at prayer in her cottage home, though the ribald jeers of the shameless multitude smote her ear, and the wild beasts, hungry and thirsty for her blood, were rushing forth in the madness of their fierce onset to rend her in pieces. The young man, who had all of life before him from which to choose, willingly gave up all the world had to promise him for the sake of his truthful conviction, and in the fresh buoyancy and hopefulness of youth went cheerfully to the death which he could scarcely bear, and proof against all promises of earthly rewards, made Heaven sure by his manly faithfulness!

Or to go back farther still — think what the Apostles were: John, the gentle, brave old man, ending his life with the words, "Love one another," upon his lips; Peter, the strong, rash man, crucified with his head downward, with that added agony as a kind of expiation for his denial of his master; James, the just and honest practical Christian, stoned to death by the Pharisees of Jerusalem; Paul, the fervent, zealous, catholic Apostle, refusing no labor and peril, and suffering death at the hands of Nero's executioners, for his fidelity to the truth which Christ had taught. Was there no real manliness in the character of these men? Nay, was there not the most genuine manliness?

But to find the manliest of men, we have to go to the founder of our religion — JESUS CHRIST himself. In all history there is nothing equal to that. To all womanly gentleness he joined all manly courage. To all the devotion of a saint he joined all the bravery of a hero. The most loving, the boldest, the kindest, the most forgiving, the most firm and faithful; he met all things, and endured all things, and did all things in that self-sustained, quiet, unpretentious and complete manliness which made him powerful against every influence of the world. We do not appreciate that sublime character of Christ till we make it a part of our own experience, and teach ourselves to follow in its way of manly duty. When we do so, we shall find that there is no trait of character which we are accustomed to look upon as belonging to the character of a complete, true and whole man, which can not be found in the character of Christ. Serene, calm, humble, dignified, honest, brave, pure, devoted, lovely, strong in purpose, persevering in action, benevolent, self-forgetting, noble, charitable, all the inward graces, all the outward virtues, combining to form the perfect stature of the man Christ Jesus!

O young man, if you desire to be noble, if you desire to be true, if you desire to be bold in all righteousness; if you desire to have that bravery which never flinches, and that courage which never falters in the way of truth, heed the examples which the history of manly endeavor gives, and learn from them that there is no strength, no truthfulness, no bravery, no courage, no manliness like that which is born of religious principle. I know your temptations. I know your trials. I know your disappointments. I know how soon your dreams of happiness fade. I know, too, your aspirations after better things — all your struggles with these powers of evil, that are dragging you down to earthliness and sin. I know how you desire to shake them off, and how weak the flesh is, though the spirit be willing. And though I have not passed from the years of youth, I have lived long enough to know that there is nothing which can effectually help you to suffer and to do but the power of a religious life; a recognition of dependence upon God; a constant effort to do his will; a resolute and persevering course of faithfulness to religious duty. There is no strength like a truly religious strength. There is no manliness like the manliness of religion! Prove, by your faithfulness, that there is as much now as in the days that are passed; and that you can bear as submissively, and do as bravely as any of God's bravest heroes! Manfully and modestly do the work which God demands of every earnest man, and daily duty shall become noble, and daily life a perpetual glory! Let a true spirit of religion dwell in all our hearts. Let love to God, and all God's children, guide us into all pleasant and dutiful ways. Let God's presence be our help and our support. Do temptations press? This will give you power to withstand them. Do trials and disappointments come? This will give you comfort. Does duty demand allegiance? This will make you faithful against all the world. Does death threaten, with its darkness, its sorrow and its pain, shutting out the bright prospect of future earthly happiness and good? This will deprive it of every terror, and open the prospect of blessedness brighter and more lasting than any thing which earth affords. "Eye hath not seen, nor ear heard, neither have entered into the heart of man, the glories which the Father hath prepared for them that love him." Each day adds to our experience of mingled pain and joy. Let each day add to our experience of the power which shall make both pain and joy conduce to good! Liberal and tolerant, faithful in religious work, strong in soul, though weakness seize the body, and pure in heart, let us pass our time below; and when the hour which closes all earthly scenes shall come, we shall be ready to pass onward to the life above, rich in all manly experience, and having bravely done our work. God grant that we may hear the Father's voice speaking to our hearts, "Well done, good and faithful servant, enter thou into the joy of thy Lord!"

III. Let me briefly state what I think the character of a young man's religion should be. 1. It should be a matter of principle. Young men, before character is formed, act generally from impulse; and a young man's impulses are generally right. But when these impulses are affected by a religious excitement, he is too apt to make his religion a mere impulse. Thus carried away, perhaps by the influence of his generous sympathies, he may feel himself swayed, as he thinks, by the sweetest and holiest emotions. Without stopping to question himself, he believes himself acted upon by the spirit of true religion. He becomes zealous; he becomes alert and active; he hurries into the Church. But after the influence of the excitement is over, and he is left with himself to combat with his temptations and his doubts, he finds that he is far weaker than he thought. His religion is on the surface and shallow. It has not reached down into his soul and become the controlling power of his life. It began with an unnatural excitement, and continued just as long as that continued, and no longer, and it leaves him a disappointed, sad, disheartened man. If he continues in the Church, he is too apt to become a hypocrite. If he leaves it he falls into skepticism; and so he lives, with perhaps an open profession of religion, and an observance of its forms, but with a secret repudiation of its sanctions. I think this to be a fair statement of the condition of that man who allows his religion to be one of impulse merely, and to grow by reason of some transient influence of temporary religious excitement. Let the young man calmly form himself; grow in silent self-communings; make his religion one of strong, genuine, undying principle, that it may sweeten his affections; that it may purify his thoughts; that it may control his words; that it may direct all his actions; that he may feel, think, say, do, in all circumstances, what that principle directs him to do. The mushroom grows in a night. It decays as quickly. The brave old oak toughens and matures through a century of conflict with the storm, and repose in the grateful sunshine. True religion grows like the oak rather than the mushroom, by a lifetime's work. So let the young man grow in religion by daily faithfulness; so let him erect the structure of his character by persevering labor. Thus he is not building his religion upon the shifting sands of worldly policy; of uncertain impulse; of sympathetic excitement; but upon the broad, strong, eternal rock of truth. Then wherever he may be, in the church or out of it; in prosperous or adverse fortunes, in quiet or in action, in life or in death, he is the true religious man.

2. A young man should be liberal and catholic in his religious principles. While he should have distinct religious opinions of his own, and should hold fast to them through all vicissitudes of his life — standing alone, if necessary, satisfied that if he has a real truth, the world will come round to him in time — he should also be tolerant of differences of opinion in others. Let him remember that men can not all think alike upon any subject, and that, upon a subject like this, which belongs to the deepest experience of our nature, uniformity of belief is particularly impossible. While he is intolerant of all that has the appearance of evil in the moral conduct of men, injustice, wrong, oppression, falsehood, vice, let him be tolerant of all that wears the appearance of truth, believing that others are as sincere as he, and that he can have no right to censure what is honestly and sincerely held as true. I can not believe altogther in the maxim, that we should agree to disagree; but that we should agree to discuss our disagreements in friendship and love. We all have some truth; and it is for the benefit of the Christian world that every shade of Christian doctrine should

find its expression. Only let us hold fast our allegiance to Him who is the common teacher of us all! Let us be no bigots. Bigotry should ever be a stranger to the young man's heart and head; but with tolerant faith let us do our work in life, with a community of philanthropic labor, and a community of active, practical duty, in all Christian spirit and in all Christian works, as Christian men should.

3. The young man should be generous in his religion; welcoming truth from whatever source it may come; reading God's wisdom and love in all the works of his hand, imprinted on the earth and sky — each plant and flower, each sun and star, bearing the impress of Divinity — reading it in the lives of holy men, who have spoken as they were moved by the Holy Spirit; in the life of Jesus Christ, teaching us all of God's fatherhood, and our own great Brotherhood; reading it in the best experience of our own souls, as they have looked up with reverential eye to the Father of all truth, and received the inspiring influences which he always sends!

4. He should be honest in his religion; receiving it with all candor, and living it with all truthfulness. Let him free himself from all cant, and all hypocrisy, and all falsehood. Let him profess nothing which he does not thoroughly believe. It is a sad thing for a young man, if he attempts to be false to God and his conscience; if he can accustom himself, for the sake of peace with his friends and kindred, or for fear of the

consequences to himself, to subscribe to opinions which in his heart he rejects; if he chooses his religious belief from any cause but a conviction of its truth; because it is fashionable, or because it may be more profitable to himself. No man can rise to the full stature of his manhood "out of the ruins of his violated truth;" and no young man is safe in moral life, whose religious life is not thoroughly honest.

5. Finally, he should always keep himself loyal to the spirit of truth. There is nothing in all this universe which can serve its stead. There is nothing so great, so powerful, so full of good. He that enters into the service of truth, never letting himself loose from its sanctions, never allowing falsehood to warp his inclinations, or prejudice to weaken his obedience, is the man who best serves his fellow-men and God. In the apochryphal book of the 1st of Esdras, it is related that Darius, king of Persia, having made a great feast, called together all the princes of his kingdom. Three young men, of the king's body guard, wrote each a sentence and gave it into the hand of the king, that he might judge the wisdom of their writing. The first wrote, "Wine is the strongest;" the second wrote, "The king is the strongest;" the third wrote, "Woman is the strongest, but above all things truth beareth away the victory." In explaining their different propositions, the first declared, "How exceeding strong is wine! it causeth all men to err that drink it!" The second declared, that as all things were obe-

dient unto the king, the king was the mightiest, for he had dominion over them. The third declared, that as woman controlled the king himself, she was stronger than all the rest. "But," he continued, "'is he not great that maketh these things? Therefore, great is the truth, and stronger than all things. Wine is wicked, the king is wicked, women are wicked, all the children of men are wicked; in their unrighteousness they shall perish. As for the truth, it endureth and is always strong; it liveth and conquereth forevermore. With her there is no accepting of persons or of rewards; but she doeth the things that are just, and refraineth from all unjust and wicked things; and all men do well like her works. Neither is her judgment in any unrighteousness; and she is the strength, kingdom, power and majesty of all ages. Blessed be the God of Truth!' And all the people shouted, 'Great is truth, and mighty above all things!'"

Such is the nature and manliness of a true religious character. Let it be your constant effort to grow in all its virtues and in all its power. Let it go with you into your homes, and it will consecrate every pure affection, and make every labor a disinterested and generous work for those who there depend upon you for their welfare. Let it go with you into your social life, and it shall make you always true and faithful to the great interests of humanity, which are intrusted to your care and direction. Let it go with you into your business, and there give you that complete integrity of purpose and act, that genuine honesty and manly truth, which make the business relations of mankind the great forces of human civilization; which make all the toil of life a glorious labor for all human good. Let it be with you in your hours of relaxation and rest, and every pleasure shall be enhanced, and the enjoyments of life shall have the relish which innocence and gratitude always furnish. Let it go with you into your politics, and it shall save you from all partisan slavery, from all prejudice, from all commendation of injustice; giving you in all relations, in all circumstances, in all conditions of life, the character of a true, independent, faithful man of God!

And now, my brothers, I can not bring this course of lectures to a close, without a word of acknowledgment. I thank you for the kind attention which you have given me, and the candid hearing which I feel I have received. I have spoken with the utmost frankness, as becometh speech between man and man. I have undertaken not so much the office of an adviser, as the duty of a friend, and if you have not agreed with all I have said, I know you will accord me the credit of having spoken honestly, sincerely and heartily. Claiming the privilege of friendship, I have endeavored not to abuse it. I am sorry now that our course is ended. I shall miss this oft-recurring meeting, and your waiting and cheerful attendance. Let me hope that our three months' work has not been useless; that my words have not been spoken in vain. If there has been any thing wrong and false, pray forget it, if you can. Let it fall and die. If any thing true and right has been said, receive and heed it well. Let it inspire you to all noble and truthful action, and let us all strive together to be true, sincere, upright, manly men! And so, I bid you a friendly and affectionate farewell!

ADDRESS

AT THE ANNUAL EXAMINATION

OF THE

NORTH-GRANVILLE FEMALE SEMINARY,

JULY 29, 1857.

In closing the exercises of the week, by addressing the members and friends of the Institution, the occasion itself, and the audience before me, furnish the appropriate subject for the brief remarks which it becomes my privilege to offer. I therefore ask your attention to a few thoughts upon the Position and Privilege of Woman, her Claims, Demands and Duties.

Among the results wrought out in the progress of civilization, none can be more noticeable, and, indeed, none is more beneficial than the gradual advance in opinion respecting the rightful position of woman. It is a long step forward from the condition of a slave to man's caprices and his sensual passions, to that of the companion of his life, sharing his best thoughts and feelings, doing a portion of his work, and helping him solve the great problems of human welfare. It has

19 *

been a step attended with many struggles — which, indeed, are not yet finished — and whose progress has been marked with defeats as well as victories. It has not been the least of the triumphs of the Christian religion, that it has succeeded in lifting woman out of her degradation, and placing her upon that level with man where both may labor "together with God," in the promotion of all human good. To illustrate the point which I here make, let me recur to the condition of woman under the civilization of the past.

In the countries of the East, the position of woman was servile. The laws of ancient Egypt, the customs of the people, and the habits of domestic life, alike reduced woman far below the place of man. Yet Egypt was the most refined and humane of ancient nations. And if there woman was compelled to bear the heaviest burdens, to perform the most laborious work, to suffer exclusion from all but the menial offices of the Temple service, and to endure the ignominy which is always incident to polygamy, we may well imagine what would be her fate among nations where humanity and refinement were unknown. India had no better place for woman. There, too, she must be the slave of man. Beside the oppressive system of caste, there was the cruel exercise of superior might to degrade her. Man was the lord of creation, and even in that vague realm of the future, to which the thoughts of the pious Hindoo sometimes turned, her condition was determined by the degree of servility which characterized her devotion to her husband in the present. China did not hesitate to deny even the possession of a soul to woman — the last degradation to which any human being can descend. Even among the Chinese at the present day, this opinion is openly declared. In a recent book of travels, written by a French missionary to that people, an account is given of an interview, which the writer enjoyed, with a Chinese of some importance, that may serve to show in what opinion woman is now held. "I have heard you say," said the Chinaman, "that people become Christians to save their souls. Is that it?" "Yes," replied the missionary, "that is the object we propose to ourselves." "Then what can women become Christians for?" "What for? to save their souls, like men." "But they have no souls," said he, stepping back and folding his arms, "women have no souls. You can not make Christians of them." The missionary endeavored to remove his scruples upon this point. The very notion tickled his fancy so much that he laughed with all his might. "Nevertheless," said he, "when I go home I will tell my wife that she has got one. She will be a little astonished, I think." Still the same writer declares, that some Chinese women have faint hopes of a future life. They endeavor to find some relief for their sufferings in the doctrine of metempsychosis. They have formed a sect called Abstinents, and by the exercise of extreme austerity, they believe they will secure a life in the future, as men. "They promise themselves, doubtless," he drily remarks, "ample compensation after their metempsychosis; and it would not be, perhaps, a very hazardous conjecture, that some of them enjoy a little the idea of the vengeance they will take upon their husbands, when they shall be transformed into men." We can conceive of no degradation more painful and cruel, than that which must result to any class of human beings from a denial to them of an immortal soul.

Among the nations of the West, though woman occupied a somewhat better position, she yet was not removed from her condition of servitude. The treatment of woman in Greece has been made the subject of a panegyric too fulsome to be true. For, though Greece was almost the only country of its time where a man was the husband of but one wife, yet the position of that wife was by no means an enviable one. The debasement of her sex still belonged to her. As a maiden, she was subject to be sold by her father or brother as a slave. As a wife, she was liable to be divorced by her husband, and given by him to another man. Moreover, she was denied participation in her husband's feasts and entertainments, where, beside, she had the mortification of knowing that the vile and vicious had free intercourse. The virtuous wife was no fit companion to her Grecian husband. The licentious Hetæræ usurped her place. The accomplished historian, Grote, gives the following painful testimony to the inferiority of Grecian women: "The free citizen women of Athens lived in strict, and almost oriental recluseness, as well after being married as when single; every thing which concerned their lives, their happiness, or their rights, was determined or managed for them by male relatives; and they seemed destitute of all mental culture and accomplishments. Their society presented no charm nor interest, which man accordingly sought for in the company of the class of women called Hetæræ, or Courtesans, who lived a free life, managed their own affairs, and supported themselves by their power of pleasing." These, and not the wives who presided over the much lauded homes of Greece, were the honored and cherished companions of the poets, the orators, the philosophers, and the statesmen of this cultivated but dissolute nation. Aspasia and Theodote may be considered the type of the best of their class; accomplished, brilliant and fascinating, but, alas, too frail. In later times, woman received more respect. The picture of the beautiful, pure, virtuous and learned Hypatia has come down to us, in the history of the period, and shows us how a woman can successfully maintain a position of influence and respect. Her terrible death lies at the door of the Christian Church. For she was literally torn in pieces, by a frenzied and fanatical mob of monks and devotees, with the sanction, if not under the immediate direction of the Christian Bishop of Alexandria.

Among the Romans, woman fared but little better than among the Greeks. "In the first ages," says Gibbon, "the father of a family might sell his children, and his wife was reckoned in the number of his children; the domestic judge might pronounce the death of the offender, or his mercy might expel her from his house; but the slavery of the wretched female was hopeless and perpetual, unless he asserted, for his own convenience, the manly prerogative of divorce. The warmest applause has been lavished on the virtue of the Romans, who abstained from this privilege for five hundred years; but the same fact evinced the unequal terms of a connection, in which the slave was unable to renounce her tyrant, and the tyrant was unwilling to relinquish his slave. When the Roman matrons (at a later period) became the equal and voluntary companions of their lords, a new jurisprudence was introduced, that marriage, like other partnerships, might be dissolved by the abdication of one of the parties. In three centuries of prosperity and corruption, this principle was enlarged to frequent practice and pernicious abuse. Passion, interest and caprice suggested daily motives for the dissolution of marriage, and the most tender of human connections was degraded to a transient society of profit and pleasure."

Among nations which claimed to have a better theory of life, we find but little improvement upon the condition of the much injured sex. The Hebrews, in common with their Eastern neighbors, practiced polygamy almost without restraint, and polygamy is always an indignity and wrong to woman. While it defiles the purest affections of the heart in the individual life, it is always the exponent of barbarism in social life. It is the unmistakable evidence of the inferiority of her whose condition is the sure index of the character of human civilization. The Old Testament is full of allusions to the inferiority of woman. Almost always she is a being to be despised. Even in later times the reproach is not removed. The Jew, catching the spirit of his ancestor, in his morning prayer, thanks God that he did not make him a Gentile, a slave, or a woman. The Jewish woman had little to expect from her husband and her master, among her own countrymen. She had less, if she should fall into the hands of the Gentiles. The Book of Esther gives us a glimpse of the condition of affairs at the court, and in the time of Ahasuerus, King of Persia. The shameful repudiation of Vashti, because she would not sacrifice her womanly modesty at the drunken behests of her lord; the still more shameful exhibition of women at court, that the king might select from among them the mistress of his harem; the certainty of the fate of Vashti, if not a worse one, for Esther, if the king had not deigned to show, in her behalf, the royal clemency, are but so many indications of the treatment which women then were compelled to undergo. The reproduction of those times is to be found to-day in the cruel customs which sanction the publie sale of the beautiful females of Georgia and Circassia, and which have spread over the East the tokens of woman's degradation and woman's woe; and in that vile system of Mormonism which seeks to perpetuate in our own land, under the guise of religion, the worst evils of the barbarism of the past!

I am aware that there are qualifications to be made to the statements which I have here put forth. I remember the women of the Bible who vindicated the freedom, and in some instances the superiority of their sex. The sagacious wisdom of Deborah, the heroic daring of Judith, the sweet simplicity of Ruth, can never be forgotten. I remember that Semiramis sat upon the throne of Assyria, and made her reign memorable in all Eastern annals — that in later times Zenobia swayed a wise and powerful sceptre in Palmyra, queen city of the desert. Venus was not the only female divinity of the Greeks. The sage Minerva and the chaste Diana had divine honors given them; and bountiful Ceres, too, sweet goddess of the fields. I recall to mind the virtue of Roman matrons, proverbial in history, the sublime self-devotion of Lucretia, the noble bearing of Cornelia, the mother of the Gracchi. Socrates, indeed, wisest and most manly of all the Grecian sages, might say — and it was because he was the wisest and most manly that he did say it — "the female sex are nothing inferior to ours, excepting only in strength of body, or perhaps in steadiness of judgment." Let us never forget this noble declaration of the noble heathen! But his great disciple, Plato, gave utterance to the more prevailing sentiment, when he declared that "man, if he misuse the privileges of one life, shall be degraded into the form of a woman" in the other! Exceptional cases there may be, but they are more prominent and noticeable because they are exceptional, and serve but to prove the proposition that woman is indebted to the influence of the Christian religion for what of freedom, what of good, what of power and privilege she now enjoys. It is Heathenism that degrades her; it is Christianity alone that elevates her to her true place.

This elevation, however, was not accomplished without great struggle. The old prejudices, which had become consolidated into institutions, could not easily be extinguished, and old customs, become fortified in law, could not easily be abrogated. But when Jesus made woman his companion and friend, when Paul declared that in Christ Jesus there was neither male nor female, and found in woman his best and most efficient co-worker in teaching and living the Christian truth, the movement was begun which is to end in the complete emancipation of woman from every species of thraldom that oppression may devise, in the acknowledgment of her equality with man in every noble enterprise and in every worthy work; in the recognition of her claim to a rightful "communion of love and labor" in the interests of Humanity, Civilization, and the Progress of mankind! What a pure piety; what a saintly devotion that was which adorned the early ages of Christian History! What heroism, that faced the torture, the arena, the stake, the cross itself, without blenching, and showed how strong a heart beat within a maiden's breast! What courage shone out upon a mother's face, and told how faithfully woman could live; how bravely she could die in defense of the truth, which filled and inspired her; all the weakness of body made strong in the power of a devoted soul! Later ages, too, have borne witness to the best traits of womanly character. The Roman Church, with that rare faculty of appropriation which distinguishes all its practical movements, has seized upon the peculiar qualifications of woman for benevolent and humane enterprise, and in the Sisters of Charity, and other kindred organizations, has done much to redeem its character, and command the gratitude of the world. Indeed, it has been seriously declared, that one reason why that church calls into its fold so many carefully educated women, is because of "the power it gives them to throw their energies into a sphere of definite utility, under the control of a high religious responsibility." Still, as benevolence belongs to no one sex, or to no one religious name, but is the product of the Christian truth, operating in the hearts of all human beings, so it is confined to no one branch of the Christian Church. Among the ranks of Protestant believers, there have been women —real Sisters of a world-wide Charity—whose lives make us proud to belong to the same great family with themselves. Need I mention such women as Elizabeth Fry, bringing the presence of Christian love into that English prison, which was truly described by one of her friends as a very "den of wild beasts?"—

"She sought her way through all things vile and base,
And made a prison a religious place,
Fighting her way — the way that angels fight
With powers of darkness — to let in the light."

As Dorothea Dix, providing, with a pertinacity which is only born of true philanthropy, a home for the indigent insane in nearly every State of the Union! As she who stands out before all the rest in our day, uniting energy with gentleness; calm perseverance against difficulties, with womanly weakness; the highest education and the most cultivated refinement, with complete devotion to the menial service of the sick, the maimed, and the helpless; showing to the world, in her illustrious example, how the very noblest souls can perform the very humblest duties, and still be noble; that pure heroine of the Crimean war, Florence Nightingale! Such instances as these, and they are not isolated in their spirit, though they may be in their practical results, assure us that woman deserves the position to which Christianity has raised her; that she was not created to be a slave; that she was not created even to fill a station of inferiority; that she was created to stand side by side with man, equal with him, though different in her characteristics; and able with him to work in the great cause of Humanity, God and Truth!

"The honest, earnest man must stand and work,
The woman also."

The progress of civilization is but the gradual recognition of universal truth, and its application to universal life. Where the feminine element of truth is disregarded and ignored, there must be an imperfect civilization. Yet, in the human heart is still the ideal of truth, and if it does not at once become real, it still strives to find expression in some way. Through the lives and acts of those who become the leaders of mankind, the truth speaks, and the artist, the poet, the man of genius, in whatever calling, looks beyond the present and the real, into the future and ideal, and constructs his Utopia, peopling it with the beings of his own creation. The future makes it real, if the present fails. In such a case as this of woman, there is the same looking forward, and if mankind in general do not recognize her worth, those who are above mankind discern the truth of her life. May this not be the reason why she finds so prominent a place in poetry, in sculpture, in art! May it not be, even as expressed among barbarous men, a foreshadowing of what is to be in the time to come? See how, in art, Civilization, Virtue, Love, Liberty, have taken the female form in their expression. It is as woman that these shine from the canvas, or speak from the marble. See how the genius of the artist recognizes the feminine principle of life. It is as woman that he would personify this, not as the rough, strong man. It is woman that treads upon the serpent of evil; that breaks the chains of cruel power; that arms herself, not with the sword, but with the palm-branch — the sceptre, as it is the weapon of peace. She fills the earth with plenty. She covers the sea with the white sails of commerce. She teaches the world of men the science and the art of human life. Is this accidental, this almost involuntary personification, in a female form, of the virtues, the best powers, and the great principles of human progress? In the ways of Providence, nothing is accidental, and it is a significant evidence of the power, which belongs to the truth, of breaking through all the errors and prejudices of men, and making, as it were, an unconscious manifestation of its presence. Let us accept it as the assurance of a position to woman, as the equal and companion of man; as his instructor even, in the graces of life; as his director in paths of wisdom; as his friend and teacher in the ways of truth and peace. The age of freedom has dawned upon the world. It is well that it is an age of Christian freedom.

It is woman's privilege, that in our day, the position which I claim for her under Christianity, is becoming so fully recognized. So much light has been shed upon all the subjects connected with human welfare, as to preclude the idea that, however tenacious the opinions of the past may be in retaining their hold upon the public mind, there can ever be a return to those opinions. To-day, in our own land, beneath these overarching skies which are the dome of God's great Temple, we rejoice to feel that God's great truth can not be stayed in its progress, and that what he has said, and what Christ has declared, and what the saintliest lives have borne witness to, can not be falsified by feeble prejudice and foolish pride! Not to one sex alone belongs the privilege of culture, and the opportunity of work. Human nature is the same in both sexes. The same human heart beats within the breasts of both alike. The same human wants need supply. The same human weakness needs strength. The same human infirmities call for help. Not that I would be understood as saying that there is no difference in the mental and spiritual organization of both, and no difference in the line of work. The very distinction which we make, in the terms manly and womanly, as applied to character, would forbid such a statement. But, while we make a difference, we are not therefore necessitated to deny an equality. Because man may be fitted to do one kind of work, and woman another, it does not follow that man's work is better, though it may be of a rougher and more practical kind. The feeble and more ideal and more spiritual is as much needed, and the soul of an action must give that action life. The outward life is the form; the inward the substance. Is it not a better philosophy to believe that each sex is dependent to some extent upon the other, and that it is by mutual help, that both are benefited? Both have been placed here to labor for each other's good, and the labor is best performed, not by dividing, but by uniting it.

Standing, then, equal with man, and possessing equal privilege, what are the demands of woman? The language which we use respecting her suggests the demands which she has to make. We speak of her as the ornament, the genius, the presiding, animating, enlivening spirit of Home. There she is the equal, the companion of man. As the motive power of that simple, underlying, yet strongest force of our civilization, she claims to be educated for that position, that she may best and most effectually exercise that power. It is not too much to say, that the civilization of a people is determined by the character of that people's homes. Look over our own land. Trace the influence of Home life, as it runs in every direction over the country. See how our own blest and beloved New-England owes her prosperity, her virtue, her intelligence, her high-toned, wide-spread power to the homes of her children! What missionaries of truth and wisdom over all the land — over all the world indeed — have gone out from their midst to carry with them the spirit that breathes through a New-England home. Never could New-England be what she is, were it not for the purity and love that find a dwelling-place upon her soil. That soil is sterile, the climate is unsteady, the way of life is hedged and filled with difficulty; but beneath an unpropitious sky, and in contention with hostile elements, have been reared the men and women that have made a community famous over all the globe. The old Puritan, stern and harsh though he may be called by his more pliant descendants, narrow even and mistaken though he may be thought, had still that far-sighted wisdom, and that sagacious virtue, which told him — for our lasting good — that a mighty empire could only be built securely, by having for the corner-stone of its foundation, a true and Christian Home!

It is but a truism to say, that woman does most toward making home what it should be. It is easy to conceive how great an influence was created upon the subsequent history of New-England, by the simple fact that the early settlers brought with them their wives and children. And certainly, to preserve this empire which they have bequeathed to us; to send down, unimpaired and undiminished, to future generations, the blessings that have been sent to us, there is needed the utmost fidelity to the principles which produced them. And thus we arrive at a knowledge of the importance which a proper female education possesses, as a preserving and directing force in our civilization. Pretentious and superficial influences are not always the strongest. There is a power working underneath the surface, which may be secret and hid away, but which, after all, is the very soul and spirit of our social and national life. We have been startled, during the past year, with the occurrenee of domestic tragedies whose frequency is without a parallel in our history, and may well fill us with alarm. May we not trace a great portion of the crime which has the widest results of injury to all that is best in our American society, to a complete misunderstanding or a willful and wanton perversion of those most sacred obligations which bind the family together? We must look well to the character of our homes—to the education to which we subject ourselves — to the education which we give to those whose privilege it may be to be at once the charm, the blessing, and the bulwark of defense to domestic life. Woman demands a home education, first of all, which shall be thorough and complete, neglecting no detail of useful work, even though it be accompanied with some feeling of disgust; neglecting also nothing which tends to the adornment and the comfort — neglecting, moreover, nothing that tends to the moral and religious discipline of the household. Woman is to be at home, not her husband's servant, but her husband's companion. The fireside is to be the brighter because of her presence there. Music and art are to blend their charms to soothe the weary hours. The cultivation of the mind is to diffuse its agreeable and refining influence. While affection, confidence and purity — that culture of the spiritual nature, without which all other accomplishments are vain — are to consecrate every hour of mutual intercourse, and fill the day with blessing! How beautiful the communion of mind and heart within the circle of a true and happy home! With pure souls and gifted minds, words inspired with intelligence and winged with love, the interchange of thought and feeling may be made the source of the very highest good beneath the skies, because its source, in turn, is above the skies. Listen to Cowper, as he sweetly sings of that rare happiness, which there is in meeting with the excellence of a pure and true soul:

"When one, that holds communion with the skies,
Has filled his urn where these pure waters rise,
And once more mingles with us meaner things,
'T is e'en as if an angel shook his wings!
Immortal fragrance fills the circuit wide,
That tells us, whence his treasures are supplied.
So, when a ship, well freighted with the stores,
The sun matures on India's spicy shores,
Has dropped her anchor and her canvas furled,
In some safe haven of this western world,
'T were vain inquiry to what port she went —
The gale informs us, laden with the scent!"

There are minor matters which belong to this important part of woman's education, but which I can not dwell upon at this time. Such are habits of personal neatness — the proper treatment of servants — a practical knowledge of housekeeping — as thorough an acquaintance with the direction of the kitchen, as a completeness in the ease and grace which adorn the drawing-room and parlor, and the like. I speak of them as minor matters. But I would not thus in any way disparage their importance. They are important, far more so than we are aware. A neglect of them is a source of much of the unhappiness and discord of home. Nay, it may lead to other and worse results yet, and be the means of much evil and perhaps downright vice. That mistress of a household, who is not thoroughly cognizant of what is called housekeeping, will find many a bitter trial for herself and her family. She is wholly at the mercy of her servants, if servants she is able to have. She is unable and incompetent to manage her household work, and becomes a mere drudge, if servants she has none. The romance of early wedded life is able to pardon many short-comings and overlook many faults, but it gradually yields to such influence. An ill-kept table, untimely meals and poorly cooked food, are as fatal to sentiment as to digestion. And it is extremely difficult to discover the angel of courtship, in the unkept hair and the slatternly dress of the wife. The slightest things oftentimes give rise to serious trouble, and the most pernicious habits may grow out of such small matters as these. They have a reflex influence upon character. Many a home has been blighted, and many a man and woman made wretched for a lifetime, on account of neglect in the little things which make up so large a portion of our lives.

"It is an error to suppose that homely minds are the best administrators of small duties." As it requires Divine power to raise out of the ground the humble spire of grass, as well as to lift the mountain's sublime and awful head; as it is the same Divine art that tints the delicate hues of the flower, and paints the glories of the skies; so it requires a genuine, manly and womanly power of soul to insure fidelity to the common things of life, and the humblest offices may be beautified by the influence of love, truth and faith. I think a proper home education takes into account every thing which is connected with the benefit of all who are in that home; to make the man more manly, the woman more womanly, the children more like what the Saviour meant when he said, "Of such is the kingdom of Heaven;" to build up in all that complete independence of character which is the assurance of faithfulness in all the duties of life. Goëthe once said: "The excellent woman is she, who, if the husband dies, can be a father to the children." There is a great deal of truth in the remark, as showing how much true self-reliance and thoroughness in the accomplishments of character, are needed in woman's life, as well as that of man.

Notwithstanding the acknowledged importance of Home, I still think it is a grave error in any one to feel that the chief end of a woman's life is to be married. Marriage is not an absolute necessity of nature, and one may be a good and true woman without it. There is such a thing as self-support and self-protection, and that consciousness of helplessness and dependence which leads one to seek in marriage the only supposable means of development, is evermore to be guarded against. Certainly, that mode of speaking, prevalent among young and old, of marriage as taking a young girl "out of the market," or of single life as being still "in the market," as though woman was a subject of sale, is open to the severest reprehension.

"I would have woman," writes one, who had thought long and deeply on the character of her sex, "lay aside all thought such as she habitually cherishes, of being taught and led by men. I would have her, like the Indian girl, dedicate herself to the Sun of Truth, and go no where, if his beams did not make clear the path. I would have her free from compromise, from complaisance, from helplessness, because I would have her good enough, and strong enough to love one and all beings from the fullness, not the poverty of her being."

There was something more than a jest in Sidney Smith's wish, that his daughter might be born with but one eye, so that he might always be sure of keeping her in his own home.

And here, I can not refrain from putting in my protest against the reproach that is too often cast upon unmarried life. "Old Maid" — what a term that is upon the lips of many persons of both sexes — let us hope thoughtlessly, rather than heartlessly uttered! Yet I ask any man or woman of you all, to-day, to recall the list of your friends and acquaintances, and see if you do not find among those whom you esteem most highly, who are ornaments to their sex for their unobtrusive goodness and kindly nature, and to whom you would soonest go for counsel and consolation in times of difficulty and grief, these same unmarried women, whom the unthinking and unfeeling are so ready to deride? Do you remember a maiden aunt, or sister, whose hand was the softest, and whose touch the gentlest, in hours of pain and sickness, whose voice had the sweetest tones for you, and whose love you were most sure of, when other friendships had been broken, and selfishness or death had quenched the affections of other hearts? Do you remember a maiden friend, whose path was marked by quiet deeds of modest worth —

> "Unpublished charity — unbroken faith —
> Love that midst grief began,
> And grew with years, and faltered not with death?"

In what happy contrast does such a life as this stand to many a married life, where disgust is not latent, where strife is not unknown, and where regard and love have long been strangers! Better far a single life, than a false and miserable marriage. Independence, even with poverty, is better than dependence with the comforts of wealth, and the unhappiness of a soulless Home!

Woman's position at the present day demands a suitable education for society. I do not mean by this an education for social intercourse, so much as for social life. Though in the first respect, certainly, a proper education is needed. Woman is the leader in social intercourse, and she can make it what she chooses. Let her carry into the social circle graceful, easy manners, acquired not so much by rule, as by a gentle, loving demeanor at home and in private; a cultivated mind, a sincere heart, a righteous principle, and that genuine politeness which grows out of a pure and womanly character. A brilliant woman will always be the centre of a circle of admirers, even though she be unprincipled and heartless. A virtuous, intelligent, true woman can always attract — what is better than admiration — respect and regard, and can always exert a strong influence for good. Who would think of indulging in falsehood by her side? Who would willingly encourage folly before her? Who would countenance wrong in her presence? Who would talk nonsense to her? The very thought of such things could not abide, when she is near. Better impulses, purer thoughts, nobler feelings, fill the mind and heart, and society — using the term in its limited sense — would be the richer for her truthful life.

But a woman's duties to society are something more than those which belong to the social circle. Beyond that circle; beyond the home walls; beyond the world of fashion is another life, which asks for woman's presence to beautify and bless it. Every social evil affects woman most of all, and woman most of all should be interested in its removal. Home and the social circle affords no surer protection from its influences. True it is, that whatever distinction we may make between different classes of society, between rich and poor, between the lofty and the lowly, we have but one human nature; we are all joined to each other and dependent upon each other; the highest allied with the humblest; the richest with the poorest; the most powerful with the weakest; the most famous with the most obscure. And this fact of mutual dependence and mutual connection inculcates the duty of mutual help. No young woman ever "comes out," as the phrase is, in its true sense, or is fit to "come out," till she has learned that love and charity, and benevolence, are womanly accomplishments, as well as Christian duties!

I have said that social evils fall heaviest, in their results of woe, upon woman. She is the victim of the brutal appetite of the drunkard; of the cruel lust of the slave owner; of the inhuman passions aroused by war. Certainly, if the greatest suffering demands the greatest interest, woman, most of all, must aid in the alleviation or removal of the woes of life. She may not, indeed, wish to enter into the grim conflict with evil, but she may have a duty to perform to those who lie wounded upon the field of battle. And not only after, but before the battle, she has the privilege to inspirit and cheer on the combatants. You remember the women of our revolution. What privations they endured! What hardships they suffered! What important services they performed in behalf of the great cause of national liberty! Even the musket itself was not wholly a stranger to their hands! You remember how they sent out the husband, brother, father, friend, into the dread strife, and you can judge with how much better bravery that strife could be carried on, when the stimulus of the remembrance of loved ones at home lent vigor to the arm. How think you a coward or a traitor would have been received in those patriot homes? And has woman nothing now to do in this great revolution which is carried on in behalf of liberty and human weal? May she not make men feel that they now have homes to defend? May she not now make men heroes for truth, freedom, righteousness, justice? Let no mean coward or false traitor now find favor at her hands!

I feel that I ought, before closing this address, to say a word or two in relation to that great question of modern civilization, the occupations of woman. There can be no doubt that it is a very serious matter, affecting all the interests of social life, to determine what shall be the employments of women, and how they shall best be fitted for carrying them forward. It reaches down into the depth of all social life, and affects as no other subject can, the whole substance of our civilized state. I do not think we do wisely, when we allow prejudice, or any pre-conceived notion, to decide such a question as this for us. It demands careful thought, and the most enlightened and candid consideration. Certainly, woman, as well as man, should have freedom of choice in her selection of an occupation, and be debarred from it by no rule or custom. Even in professional and in the higher walks of literary life, she has shown her ability to acquire equal honors with man. We are glad to accept her services as teacher. We have seen how successful she may be, in any line of work in which she may engage. Even as a sailor, as is abundantly shown in the recent heroic instance of Mrs. Patten, she has proved successful in encountering the roughness of the elements, and the insubordination of rude and reckless men, with a fortitude full of the spirit of true manliness, yet without any derogation of womanly dignity. As a ruler, she has left many an illustrious record in the history of the race! As a writer, she has had few equals. As a scholar, she has exhibited unwonted genius. The best Universities in Italy, in the fifteenth century, were proud to enroll among their professors, and to load with academic honors, the learned women of the time. The scientific world acknowledges its indebtedness to her power of acute perception and accurate description. She has stood at the bed-side of the sick and dying as nurse and as physician too, and by her kind and careful treatment has smoothed the way of many a weary hour of pain; while, as the teacher of religion, she has brought the consolations and strengthening precepts of the Gospel to aid the tempted, to encourage the harassed and doubting, and to solace the heart worn with the cares and troubles of life.

> "Day unto day her dainty hands
> Make life's soiled temples clean,
> And there's a wake of glory where
> Her spirit pure hath been.
> At midnight through that shadow land,
> Her loving face doth gleam:
> The dying kiss her shadow, and
> The dead smile in their dream."

I think we should pursue toward woman, in this instance, as in every other, the most respectful and the most generous course. Allowing her freely to choose the occupation which best suits her capacity, her inclination and her convenience, if it be an honest and honorable one, we would encourage her in it, to be faithful. Believing that the enlargement of her sphere of action will be for the improvement of her character, and, indeed, of all social life, we would demand for her a more regardful estimation. We have no right to sneer and ridicule her ways of life, if they are good, for sneers and ridicule are cowardly and unmanly. Let woman choose her occupation as she will, and let her be encouraged to success in it. This is what a true man would always say. But, whether we say it or not, woman will generally have her own way. There is a great deal of significance in the old, homely couplet:

> " When a woman will, she will, you may depend on 't;
> And when she won't, she won't — and there 's the end of 't."

Let us accept its truth, and make the best of it!

Ladies and gentlemen, the subject extends itself in such various directions, and over so wide a field of thought and discussion, that I have hardly been able to do more than offer a few imperfect suggestions. So intimate a connection has it with all social welfare, as to demand the most thorough examination, and while I could not hope to exhaust it, I still desired to present it to your attention. I leave it now to your own reflections. The position of woman, rightfully considered, is so noble, her influence so powerful, her work so wide, her duties so commanding, as to demand for herself and them the most faithful consideration. This institution, with all its advantages for moral, social, and literary culture, attests the appreciation in which you hold the subject of the development of womanly character and mind. May it long remain a monument to the beneficence of its founders, and disseminate, far and wide, the blessings of sound instruction, good morals, and religious life!

Young Women, accept the position which I have held up before you, and improve the means which here are offered for educating yourselves, to work upon human life to the very best advantage for yourselves and others. Look out upon the world. Life is somewhat more than a scene of gay frivolity and fashionable display. It is a scene on which the purest virtues, and the noblest accomplishments of character may find their theatre of action. To beautify Home, to purify Social Life, to exert a humanizing and elevating influence upon all our Civilization—this is now your work. When you leave school walls behind you, your education is by no means finished. All along your way of life, you will find schools and schoolmasters, and from every hour's experience shall come lessons of renewed instruction, and encouragements to renewed fidelity.

Let there come with them, too, mingling with every event of life, and

> "Blending the soul's sublimest needs
> With tasks of every day,"—

the lessons and influences of a true religion. Let its spirit pervade the life, like the warm breezes of Spring upon the earth, entering every nook and cranny of the soul — melting the ice which selfishness freezes around the heart — softening every harsh feature of the character with its gentle touch — breathing through the whole soul its fresh and genial airs. A pure religion, when it enters into a man's soul, makes him a hero in duty — when it enters a woman's, it makes her a saint in life. There is heroism in saintliness — heroism of the brightest kind. The pages of Christian History have no more illustrious examples of self-devotion, than were exhibited by the female martyrs of the Church! What higher heroism can there be than that which had for its scene of action the hospitals of the East, and, still more recently, the plague-stricken cities of the South? What higher heroism can there be than that which shows itself in patiently suffering, in bravely working for human good, and in that sublime self-sacrifice which may glorify each humblest woman's heart? The noblest ladies of Europe are proud to bear the name of Sisters of Charity and Mercy. But there is a nobler name still — and that is possible to achieve by every youthful maiden now before me, which in its satisfying influence, will make life all beautiful and rich — the name of CHRISTIAN WOMAN!

PLAIN WORDS.

ERRATA.

Theater and *center* when they occur, should be *theatre* and *centre*.

Page 45. 17th line from top, insert *evils* after *those*.

Page 56. 4th line from bottom, read *strong* for *they*, and *is* for *be*.

Page 68. 10th line from bottom, insert *our* after *carry*.

Page 69. 3d line from top, read *as* for *or*.

Page 162. Last line, read *feet* for *foot*.

Page 170. 5th line from bottom, read *free* for *true*.

Page 190. 14th line from bottom, read *his* for *their*.

Page 195. 13th line from bottom, read *there* for *then*.

Page 197. 13th line from bottom, read *school-man* for *school-room*.

Page 239. 13th line from top, read *unkempt* for *unkept*.

www.ingramcontent.com/pod-product-compliance
Lightning Source LLC
LaVergne TN
LVHW050513100826
845148LV00002B/325

* 9 7 8 1 4 2 5 5 2 1 7 5 2 *